日本語

Kimono ③

Sue Burnham · Yukiko Saegusa · Michael Sedunary

Photography by
Michael Sedunary
Illustrations by
Ross Gray
Edited by
Helen McBride
Designed by
Josie Semmler

Consultants
Robyn Spence-Brown
Hiroshi Honda

Produced with the assistance of
The Japan Foundation

CIS Educational

First published 1992 by CIS Educational

Reprinted 1997 by CIS•Heinemann
a division of Reed International Books Australia Pty Ltd
22 Salmon Street, Port Melbourne, Victoria 3207
Telephone (03) 9245 7111
Facsimile (03) 9245 7333
World Wide Web http://www.heinemann.com.au
Email info@heinemann.com.au

Offices in Sydney, Brisbane, Adelaide and Perth.
Associated companies, branches and representatives around the world.

2006 2005 2004 2003 2002 2001 2000 1999 1998 1997
15   14   13   12   11   10   9   8   7   6   5

© Reed International Books Australia Pty Ltd 1992

Edited by Helen McBride
Designed by Josie Semmler
Photography by Michael Sedunary
Illustrated by Ross Gray
Typeset on Apple Macintosh

Printed in Australia by Impact Printing Pty Ltd

National Library of Australia Cataloguing-in-Publication data

Burnham, Sue.
  Kimono. Level 3.

  ISBN 0 949919 97 7.

  1. Japanese language – Textbooks for foreign speakers –
  English. I. Saegusa, Yukiko. II. Sedunary, Michael. III. Title.

495.682421

もくじ

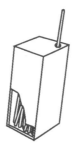

Students and teachers familiar with the first two levels of this course will immediately appreciate that *Kimono 3* represents another stage in the evolution of the *Kimono* method.

The photo-stories

The most striking feature of this development is the progression from まんが to photo-stories. These combine photographs with speech bubbles and captions to provide a graphic portrayal of life as lived by a group of five Japanese teenagers. The image of the grimly serious Japanese student is turned on its head as these young people take us shopping, out on a date, to a restaurant, home to a private karaoke party and generally allow us to share in their very full and interesting lives. These students are not ground down by the demands of their school-work; they have a real sense of fun, giving plenty of scope for the humour which has been such an important part of the *Kimono* course so far.

The students involved live in Odate, a town in the Tohoku area of Japan. They introduce us to other family members who are involved in activities ranging from part-time jobs to a dog show. The scene of the action broadens at times as other photo-stories give the chance to young 'guest stars' to show us different parts of Japan. With them we visit Kyoto, Hiroshima and Miyajima, for example.

The cultural background

The photo-stories are obviously an excellent vehicle for integrating Japanese language and culture. In *Kimono 3* the distinction between the two becomes blurred as language is always presented in the context of the local way of life.

The cultural information, both photographic and textual, provided by the photo-stories is supplemented by some articles in English on different aspects of contemporary Japanese lifestyle. These include such diverse topics as traditional religious practices, karaoke, flower viewing and Children's Day. Simone even felt obliged to contribute one last letter, on the problems facing the exchange student readjusting to life at home.

In each case, cultural background material is closely related to the language topic being dealt with in the unit.

The format

This third level makes use of a freer, more flexible format: the number of photo-stories varies from unit to unit and sometimes these are preceded, rather than followed by, the related いいましょう. This flexibility of format allows for greater variety in the presentation of language points without sacrificing the progression from simpler to more complex.

The language

Kimono 3 ventures boldly into a region where many others have feared to tread: Japanese *plain style* speech. This is *real* Japanese, the language spoken in informal family and friendship situations. This book also tackles the distinctions between written and spoken Japanese, between informal and polite speech and between male and female speech.

Obviously, it is impossible to 'legislate' for something as fluid and variable as plain style Japanese speech. Students are simply provided with one model that will enable them to talk as naturally as possible with Japanese students of a similar age.

Since intonation is such an important aspect of plain style speech, the *Kimono 3* tapes will be an invaluable aid in its presentation. The *Kimono 3 Workbook* will play an important role in giving students continuing practice in です/ます patterns.

Students are exposed to a wide variety of language situations and the styles appropriate to these situations. There is a move to broaden the language base from the students' personal lives to include more 'transactional' language: as well as expressing their attitudes and feelings and discussing their experiences and plans, students learn the language of making arrangements and obtaining goods, as well as seeking and giving directions.

Teachers will need to continually remind students of the importance of suiting their speech style to the particular demands of different language situations.

The authentic materials

The materials reproduced in *Kimono 3* include menus, maps, advertising brochures, TV guides, timetables, signs and department store guides. This book continues the trend, begun in the second level, of linking information presented in this material to a range of oral activities. Not only are students presented with these real life 'documents', they are given something to do with them. They are required to identify, to describe, to negotiate, to express opinions and to explain.

The grammar

The main burden of presenting the language in each unit is borne by the photo-stories and the いいましょう exercises. However, as in previous levels, grammatical explanations play an important role in underpinning the wealth of communicative material.

Where appropriate, *Kimono 3* makes use of verb tables and useful grammatical terminology. The result is that language is presented in a balanced way that is accessible to a wide range of learning styles.

The Japanese script

In *Kimono 3* it is assumed that students have mastered the *hiragana*, *katakana* and *kanji* presented in the previous levels. A further twenty-nine *kanji* have been selected for introduction at this level on the basis of their relevance to the language presented (rather than the 'simplicity' of the *kanji*). This means that there are ample opportunities for reinforcing these *kanji* throughout the text.

The *kanji* section in the textbook is for teacher and student reference only. Stroke order and practice squares are included in the *Kimono 3 Workbook*. The *Workbook* also contains handwritten examples of *kanji*.

The vocabulary

The vocabulary in *Kimono 3* is presented along with the item to which it relates. In general, words that occurred in the first two levels are not included in this text, unless they were previously treated as passive vocabulary.

In this third level, passive vocabulary is given at the foot of the relevant page to allow for minimal interruption to the reading of the passage concerned.

All vocabulary given in this book is included in the Japanese-English, English-Japanese word lists at the end of the book. The meanings given are the ones that relate specifically to the text. がいらいご are also included in these lists.

The Kimono 3 Teacher's Manual

This manual features detailed notes for teachers suggesting practical strategies to use in the day-to-day teaching of the course.

The manual also includes reproduction masters with:

· extra exercises and comprehension questions;
· dialogues as samples for the いってみましょう activities; and
· supplementary reading passages.

Kimono 3 is a multi-faceted course and requires thoughtful balancing of all the elements. The *Teacher's Manual* aims to assist teachers in the integration of the textbook, workbook and cassettes, as well as in the coordination of the various language presentations, exercises and activities.

ご協力いただいた方々

The authors wish to express their appreciation to the following people and organisations who made a contribution to this book:

Dr and Mrs M. Ishida, Mrs R. Ishida and Mrs I. Aburakawa for their generous hospitality in Japan;

Dr and Mrs T. Kogure and Mr and Mrs S. Kawate for their kind assistance;

The Principal, staff and students of Homei Senior High School, Odate;

Kumiko Arakawa, Shoji Kobayashi, Maiko Suzuki, Kimihiro Tsuya and Fumie Abe for their enthusiastic cooperation;

The management of Daikichi restaurant, Odate;

Jusco department store, Odate;

Big Echo Karaoke Studio, Odate;

Petit Gourmet restaurant, Odate;

and the people of Odate in general, who always showed great kindness and cooperation.

Most photographs used in this book were taken on location in Japan by Michael Sedunary. Exceptions to this are the photographs of Japanese students from the past (pages 4 and 5), supplied by themselves, and the two bottom photographs on page 142 which were taken at the Toki Restaurant, Melbourne, Australia.

Finally, the publishers gratefully acknowledge the companies who kindly gave their permission to use copyright material in this book. Despite every effort, the publishers were not always successful in tracing all copyright owners. Should this come to the attention of the copyright owners concerned, the publishers request that they contact them so that proper acknowledgement can be made in any reprint of this book.

Legend

The following symbols are used throughout the text and denote *female* speech, *male* speech, both *female and male* speech and where no symbol appears, *polite* speech.

例:	
	— female speech (plain)
	— male speech (plain)
	— both female and male speech (plain)
	— polite speech

まいこさんです。

きみひろくんと
しょうじくんです。

ふみえさんです。

しょうじくん
です。

くみこさん
です。

きみひろくん
です。

東北
（とうほく） is the name given to the region which includes the six
prefectures in the north of 本州
（ほんしゅう）. As well as being Japan's main
rice-producing area, the region is famous for its many national
parks, lakes, cedar forests, hot springs and ski resorts.

東北 (とうほく)

十和田湖
（とわだこ）

大館
（おおだて）

大_{だい}もんじ山

大館_{おおだて}

大館_{おおだて}は東北_{とうほく}にあります。東京_{とうきょう}から東北_{とうほく}
しんかんせんとバスで行けます。東北_{とうほく}
しんかんせんはグリーンです。
みなさん、いっしょにしんかんせんで
大館_{おおだて}へ行きましょう。

大館_{おおだて}は東北_{とうほく}のゆうめいな十和田湖_{とわだこ}のそばにあります。大館_{おおだて}の
じんこうは70000人です。あまり大きくないです。しずかなまちです。
山や川や田んぼがたくさんあります。きれいなこうえんもあります。
「大_{だい}もんじ山」のしゃしんを見てください。この「大」は
大館_{おおだて}の「大」です。

これはほうめいこうこうです。いま山田せんせいは、たいいくの
じゅぎょうをしています。

単語	
グリーン	green
そば	beside, near
じんこう	population
や	and
田んぼ	rice field
ほうめいこうこう	Homei Senior High School
じゅぎょう	class

さあ! あたらしいともだちをしょうかいします。

こんにちは。ぼくのなまえは小林昭二です。大館に
すんでいます。かぞくは五人です。父と母とおとうとと
いもうとがいます。ふゆ、よく山にスキーに行きます。
これはきょねんのスキーツアーのしゃしんです。
みんなかっこいいね!
ぼくはピンクのパーカを
きて、しろいスキーパンツを
はいています。
ぼくはほうめいこうこうの三ねんせい
です。Gぐみです。まい日、でんしゃで
がっこうに行きます。ときどきともだちの
きみひろくんとでかけます。ぼくはすしが大すきです。

> このぼうし、どう? かわいい?

はじめまして。荒川久美子です。十六さいです。
ほうめいこうこうの二ねんせいです。えい語の
クラブのメンバーです。えい語はむずかしいですが、
大すきです。かぞくは五人で父と母とあねのみほと
あにのあきらとわたしです。あにはけっこんしています。
こどもが一人います。あねは大がくせいです。そぼは
うちのそばにすんでいます。よくうちにきます。そふは
十ねんまえになくなりました。

このしゃしんを見てください。
ひまなとき、よく買いものをします。

このしゃしんはちゅうがっこうのそつぎょうしきの
しゃしんです。こうちょうせんせいといっしょに
とりました。

> わたしは
> 四さいです。

単語	
ふゆ	winter
スキーツアー	skiing holiday
〜ぐみ	...class
はじめまして	pleased to meet you
クラブのメンバー	a member of a school club
が	but
けっこんしている（しています）	to be married
大がくせい	university student
（大がく	university)
〜ねんまえ	...years ago
なくなる（なくなります）	to die
そつぎょうしき	graduation ceremony
こうちょうせんせい	school principal
ぼうし	hat

鈴木舞子です。大館にすんでいます。四人かぞくです。あにのまことは大阪にすんでいます。かいしゃいんです。

あにはえい語がじょうずです。わたしもえい語のクラブのメンバーです。けんどうもします。けんどうはおもしろいですよ。

大館のふゆはさむいですがわたしはゆきが大すきです。このしゃしんを見て...十四ねんまえにとりました。よくゆきあそびをしました。

ほうかご、よくくみこさんと買いものをします。どうぞよろしく。

オス！ぼくは津谷公博です。十七さいです。ぼくのかぞくは四人です。りょうしんといもうとがいます。ほうめいこうこうの三ねんせいです。

よくともだちとでかけます。ほうかご、ときどきおこのみやきを食べます。

たいてい、どよう日にガールフレンドのふみえちゃんとデートします。ふみえちゃんは十六さいです。かつらこうこうの二ねんせいです。とてもかわいいおんなのこです。

単語	
かいしゃいん	company employee
ゆき	snow
ほうかご	after school
オス	hi!
りょうしん	parents
おこのみやき	a kind of thick, spicy pancake containing vegetables and meat or seafood
たいてい	usually
ガールフレンド	girlfriend
（ボーイフレンド	boyfriend)
デートする（します）	to have a date
かつらこうこう	Katsura Senior High School
おんなのこ	girl
（おとこのこ	boy)

くみこさんのかぞくについて

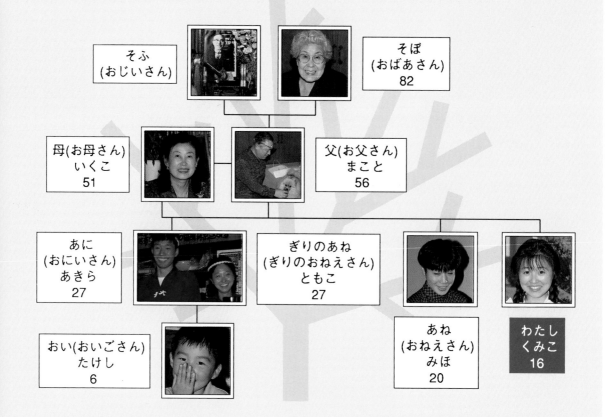

Using the examples as a guide, talk about くみこさんの かぞく.

例:
A　この人はだれですか。
B　お母さんのいくこさんです。
　　or
　　ぎりのおねえさんのともこさんです。

例:
A　おにいさんはいますか。
B　はい、います。
　　or
　　いいえ、いません。

例:
A　おねえさんのなまえは何ですか。
B　みほさんです。

A　何さいですか。
B　はたちです。

When the *Kimono* authors first interviewed くみこさん, this is what she told them about her family tree.
Use it as a model for talking with your friend about your families.

Q くみこさん、何人かぞくですか。

くみこ 五人です。

Q だれとだれですか。

くみこ 父と母とあにとあねとわたしです。

Q この人はだれですか。

くみこ あねのみほです。

Q じゃ、この人は?

くみこ ぎりのあねです。あにはけっこんしています。

Q こどもさんがいますね。くみこさんはおばさんですね。

くみこ ええ。

Q おいごさんは何さいですか。

くみこ 六さいです。

Q おばあさんがいますね。何さいですか。

くみこ そぼは八十二さいです。

Q おじいさんは?

くみこ そふは十ねんまえになくなりました。

かぞくの単語		
Your family		**Your friend's family**
りょうしん	parents	ごりょうしん
こども	child/children	こどもさん
おば	aunt	おばさん
おじ	uncle	おじさん
おい	nephew	おいごさん
めい	niece	めいごさん
ぎりの...	...in-law, step...	ぎりの...
だれとだれですか。Who is in your family?		
はたち 20 years of age		

いいましょう 二

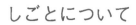
しごとについて

 一 けいかん

 二 ガイド

 三 えきいん

四  だいく

五  てんいん

 六 タクシーの うんてんしゅ

Do any members of your family have any
of the jobs pictured here or listed below?
Using the examples as a guide, talk about them with a partner.

例:
A　お父さんはどんなおしごとですか。
B　父はいしゃです。

例:
A　お母さんは?
B　母ははいしゃです。

accountant	かいけいし	housewife	しゅふ
architect	けんちくか	lawyer	べんごし
bank employee	ぎんこういん	nurse	かんごふ
company employee	かいしゃいん	...owner	...のオーナー
cook	コック	plumber	すいどうや
dentist	はいしゃ	public servant	こうむいん
doctor	いしゃ	receptionist	うけつけ
electrician	でんきや	secretary	ひしょ

大

Meaning: *big*

Readings
おお
だい

大きい・おおきい
大館・おおだて
大阪・おおさか

大学・だいがく
大好き・だいすき

小

Meaning: *small*

Readings
ちい
しょう

小さい・ちいさい

小学校・しょうがっこう

とうほくのおばあちゃん
こどもが四人だよ
ある日、こどもにあいたくて
しんかんせんでとうきょうに

くりかえし
いってらっしゃい、おばあちゃん
あんまり でかけないで
じゃ、またね、おばあちゃん
あんまりあそばないで

こどものまさきさん
トラックのうんてんしゅ
おばあちゃんつれてディスコに
オールナイトでロックンロール

くりかえし...

こどものまきこさん
バスのガイドだよ
おばあちゃんつれてパチンコに
チンジャラジャラ！おおあたりよ！

くりかえし...

こどものまさおさん
ぎんざでおまわりさん
おばあちゃんつれてカラオケに
マイクもって、がんばれれ、がんばれ！

くりかえし...

こどものまさこさん
しごとはだいくだよ
おばあちゃんつれてやきとりやに
おいしい、おいしい、99ほん！

くりかえし...

単語	
ある日	one day
あいたくて	want to see (a person)
くりかえし	chorus, repeat
でかけないで	don't go out!
あそばないで	don't play up!
つれて	take
チンジャラジャラ	the sound of *pachinko*
おおあたり	a big win
おまわりさん	neighbourhood policeman
マイクもって	holding the microphone
やきとり	pieces of chicken on skewers

一   More about particles

の

You can use の to show the connection between yourself and someone else.

e.g. あねのみほははたちです。
My older sister, Miho, is twenty.

まちでともだちのまいこさんに
あいました。
I met my friend, Maiko, in town.

You can also use の to indicate the relationship between other people.

e.g. きみひろくんはガールフレンドの
ふみえさんとでかけました。
Kimihiro went out with his girlfriend, Fumie.

や

There is more than one way of saying *and* in 日本語.

Compare these two sentences.

デパートで本とペンセットを
買いました。
I bought a book and pen-set at the department store.

デパートで本やペンセットを
買いました。
I bought a book and pen-set at the department store.

By using と in the first sentence, you are saying that you bought a book and pen-set only.
By using や in the second sentence, you are saying that you bought some other things as well.

In the introduction to 大館(おおだて) we read:

山や川や田んぼがたくさん
あります。
There are lots of mountains, rivers and rice fields (around Oodate).

There are, of course, other things around 大館, but by using や the writer is saved the job of listing them all.

が

There are also other ways of saying *but* in 日本語.

Compare these two cases.

えい語はむずかしいですが大すき
です。
English is difficult but I really like it.

えい語はむずかしいです。でも
大すきです。
English is difficult... But I really like it.

In the first case, が is used to join two parts of the one sentence.
In the second, でも is used because it begins a new sentence. You cannot begin a sentence with が.
でも has a stronger meaning than が.
It can also be translated as *however*.

二   More about まえ

In telling the time, you used まえ to indicate the number of minutes before the hour.

e.g. 八じ五ふんまえにあいましょう。
Let's meet at 5 to 8.

まえ also means *ago*. With this meaning, it is usually followed by に.

e.g. そふは十ねんまえに
なくなりました。
My grandfather died 10 years ago.

五ねんまえに日本に行きました。
I went to Japan 5 years ago.

三   はたち

Under Japanese law one becomes an adult at twenty years of age. January 15 is called *Coming-of-Age Day* and it is a national holiday. Congratulatory ceremonies are held on that day for those who turn twenty in that year.

There is also a special word to mark the age twenty. Someone who is twenty years old is said to be はたち.

ダイエット中

1

あついね。

うん、あつい。
アイスクリーム
食べたいね。

そうね。

あっ、おいしそう! 見て、あのオレンジ
アイス。モカもおいしそう。

うん。おいしそうね。

2

でも、わたし、ダイエット中...

ダイエット? ざんねんねえ。

3

じゃあ、わたし、その
オレンジアイスのシングル
ください。

はい。120円です。

4

ああ、おいしい、おいしい。

5

おいしそう！いいなあ…

6

トリプルください。

わあ！トリプル!? ダイエットは？

きょうはやすみ。ダイエットは
あしたから…

7

ああ、おいしい。

まったく…

8

一

二

四

五

六

How do the things in the pictures look to you?
Make your comments, using the example as a guide.
The words in the box below may be helpful.

おいしい　　おもしろい　　たのしい
むずかしい　　まずい　　つまらない　　よい

	例: A　おいしそうね。 B　うん、おいしそうね。
	A　おいしそうだね。 B　うん、おいしそうだね。
	A　おいしそうですね。 B　ええ／はい、そうですね。 　　or 　　ええ／はい、おいしそうですね。

These things look interesting, don't they?
Using the example as a guide, say that you would like to do them too.

	例:
	A おもしろそうね。 B うん、見たいね。
	A おもしろそうだね。 B うん、見たいね。
	A おもしろそうですね。 B ええ／はい、見たいですね。

6

あっ、あのえいが
おもしろそうだね。
見たいね。

うん、
見たいね。

7

ロマンティックだね。
ねえ、こんばんはどう?

こんばん? こんばんは
ちょっと...

すみませんが... ミスタードーナツは
どこでしょうか。

8

ミスタードーナツ
ですか。ロッテリアの
となりにあります。

とおいですか。

いいえ、とおくない
ですよ。

どうもありがとう。

いいえ。

9

10

ねえ、こんばんだめ？

ふみえ...

うん... しゅくだいが
たくさん... あのクラブの
せんぱいはどう？

あのう、すみません。

どうしたんですか。

あのう、
ロッテリアは
どこでしょうか。

ロッテリア？
いとくのまえ
ですよ。

11

ああ、そう。どうもすみません。

じゃ、土よう日は？

12

土よう日？

あっ！あのおばさん、また！

13

一 ミスタードーナツ

ロッテリア

 二 はなや

ミスタードーナツ

 三 バスてい

ロッテリア

四 こうえん

(お) しろ

五 ダッキーダック

ロッテリア

六 アートコーヒー

ル ガトー

Using the example as a guide, talk about where these places are in relation to each other. The words in the box below may be helpful.

| となり | うえ | した | まえ | うしろ | そば |

例:
A　すみませんが... ミスタードーナツはどこでしょうか。
B　ミスタードーナツですか。ロッテリアのとなりにあります。
A　どうもすみません。

In this dialogue friends are meeting in town to buy a birthday present. Make up a conversation with a partner. Decide who will be A and who will be B. A has two roles.

	バスていで						
A	すみませんが…	だいまるデパート みつこしデパート		は どこでしょうか。			
B	だいまる みつこし	ですか。	だいまる みつこし	は	マリオンえいがかん とうきょうえき	の	となり まえ そば	に
	あります。ちょっととおいですよ。							
A	バスで行けますか。							
B	ええ、	62ばん 103ばん 95ばん	の バスで行けます。いま わたしも		だいまる みつこし	に行きます。		
	いっしょに行きませんか。							
A	どうも。きょう何を買いますか。							
B	ともだちの	ディーン メリサ パット	くん さん	のバースデープレゼントです。			
	らいしゅうは	十六さい 十七さい 十八さい	のたんじょう日です。					
A	そうですか。							
	デパートのまえで							
A2	ひろこさん、 ひろしくん、	ここ!						
B	あ、	ふみこさん、 まさきくん、	おそくなってごめんね。					
	デパートの中で							
A2	あっ、この	ジャケット シャツ ベルト	はどう?	よさそうね。 よさそうだね。			
B	そう?よくないよ。	つまらないよ。 たかいよ。						
A2	じゃ、この	CD チョコレート コンピューターゲーム	は?					

B	うん、	おもしろそう おいしそう たのしそう	ね。 だね。	
	すみません...	この	CD チョコレート コンピューターゲーム	をください。

土
Meaning: *earth*
Readings
ど
土曜日・どようび

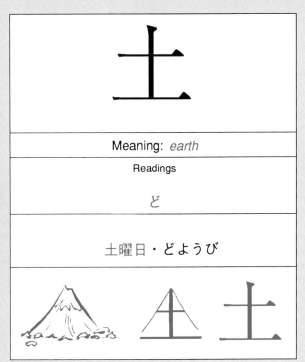

中
Meaning: *in, middle*
Readings なか ちゅう
うちの中・うちのなか
中国・ちゅうごく ダイエット中・ダイエットちゅう

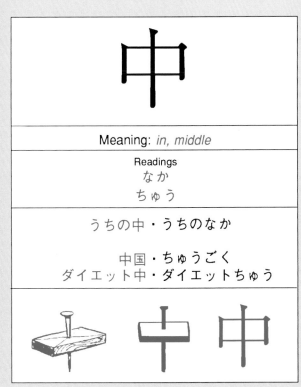

ねえ、みなさん。みなさんはおひるごはんに
いつも何を食べますか。サンドイッチ?

日本では、おべんとうを食べます。
いろいろなおべんとうがありますよ。

このおんなのこのおべんとうを
見ましょうか。おにぎりといっしょに
チキンやにくややさいやたまごを
食べます。おいしそうですね。

しんかんせんの中でも食べられます。
この人たちを見てください。

おいしい!

4

このとくべつなおべんとうは
えきべんです。えきべんはえきや
でんしゃの中で買えます。
べんりですね。

おべんとうはいかがですか。

5

6

どうぞ。

ありがとう。

こうえんでも田んぼでも
おべんとうを食べます。

7

いただきます。

さあ、みなさん。あしたの
おひるごはんにおべんとうを
つくって食べませんか。

おひるごはんに何を食べますか。

Conduct a survey among ten friends to find out what they usually have for lunch at school. You can ask about what they eat and drink, where they have their lunch and who they eat with. Draw up a table like the one below to record your responses.

ともだちのなまえ	食べもの	のみもの	どこで	だれと

When you have completed your survey, you will be able to make some general statements about the lunch habits of your friends.

e.g. たいていこうていでひるごはんを食べます。

一　おもしろそう

あのえいがはおもしろそうですね。
That film looks interesting, doesn't it?

あのみせはたかそうですね。
Doesn't that shop look expensive!

To say how something looks or appears to you, drop the final い from an い adjective and add そう.

おもしろい	おもしろそう
たかい	たかそう
おいしい	おいしそう
たのしい	たのしそう
いい	よさそう

The only exception is いい. Remember how いい changed to よかった and よくない? To say that something looks good, you say よさそうです.

e.g. このシャツはよさそうです。
This shirt looks good.

おいしそう　おいしい　おいしかった

二　食べたい

To say what you want to do, replace 〜ます on the end of a verb with 〜たい（です）

e.g. こんばんテレビが見たいです。
I want to watch TV tonight.

おひるごはんにサンドイッチが食べたいです。
I want to have sandwiches for lunch.

Notice that が is used instead of を to point out what you want to do.

Do not use the たい form when inviting someone to do something or suggesting an activity. You use the 〜ましょう or 〜ませんか form of the verb.

三　Plain speech

In 日本語, the style of speech people use depends on who is speaking and to whom they are speaking. In *Kimono 1*, you learned that you could just say おはよう to your friends and family but when you greet your teacher and adults that you don't know very well, you should say おはようございます

おはよう is an example of *plain* speech. おはようございます is an example of *polite* speech.

Most of the 日本語 you have learned up until now is polite speech. You use it when talking to people you don't know very well and in most work and school situations when speaking to people senior to you. When you are using polite speech you use です and 〜ます endings.

In *Kimono 3* you will learn plain speech. This is the informal language that family members and friends use when talking to each other.

When ふみえちゃん asked きみひろくん about the girl in the blue car, she said, あの人だれ? This is an example of plain speech. The polite version of this is あの人はだれですか。 You can see and hear that plain speech is a shorter, more direct, 'no-frills' language in which some words and some particles are dropped.

In plain speech です changes to だ or is dropped altogether.

e.g. きみひろくん says,
あのえいが、おもしろそうだね。
That film looks good, doesn't it.

Generally だ is used by male speakers. As だ is not usually a part of female speech, most female speakers drop it.

e.g. まいこさん says,
そのオレンジアイス、おいしそうね。
That orange ice cream looks good!

You will have noticed that in both of these sentences the particle は is omitted.

With い adjectives and たい form, male and female speech is the same. They both drop です. The particle が is also dropped.

e.g. あついね。
Isn't it hot!

アイスクリーム食べたいね。
I want to have an ice cream.

四 すみませんが...
どこでしょうか。

You have already used すみません to express apologies. You can also use it to express thanks.

e.g. どうぞ。
Here you are.
すみません。
Thank you. (Sorry to have put you out.)

If you add が to すみません, you indicate that you are about to ask for assistance.

e.g. すみませんが...だいまるデパートはどこでしょうか。
Excuse me, (but) could you please tell me where Daimaru department store is?

The が has a softening effect, adding a polite hesitation, an apology for the disturbance.

By using でしょうか rather than ですか when you are asking where something is, you are being more polite.

e.g. すみませんが...えいがかんはどこでしょうか。
Excuse me, (but) could you please tell me where the picture theatre is?

だいまるデパートのとなりにあります。
It's next to Daimaru department store.

どうもすみません。
Thank you.

すみませんが...

あついね。

アイスクリーム
食べたいね。

'A samurai's life is like a cherry blossom: it briefly blooms and then it falls.' So goes the old Japanese saying. You can see what it is saying about both, can't you? Both are transitory, precious, to be experienced and appreciated before they are snuffed out.

There aren't any more samurai in Japan, but the cherry blossoms still bloom every spring, and Japanese people go out of their way to sit under them, to walk under them, to admire them, to appreciate them. はなみ, flower viewing, is an established part of Japanese culture. It means making a special expedition with the purpose of experiencing the blossoms at まんかい time — that is the time when they are in full bloom. So seriously do they take it, that during the months of March and April, the televison weather report includes lines on the map of Japan — the さくらぜんせん — showing exactly where the blossoms are in まんかい.

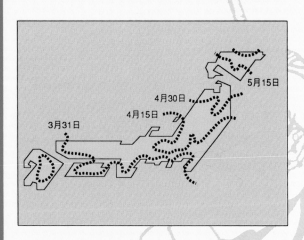

It's not just ageing romantics who do はなみ. Everybody does it, although it usually involves work or friendship groups rather than family outings. So, what do you do during はなみ? Well, you sit under the cherry trees, and you eat and drink and talk and invite other people over to eat and drink and talk. And you enjoy the arrival of spring, and you enjoy doing something that is just so Japanese.

Like most other things in Japan, はなみ can be pretty competitive. Prime blossom viewing spots are in huge demand and office juniors are often sent out at some ridiculously early hour to secure a good position in the local park. They spread the company piece of plastic and hold the fort until their workmates are free to leave the office and begin the festivities.

You arrive at your はなみ site, carrying your special はなみ おべんとう, with the rice in the shape of a cherry blossom. You enjoy the fact that there is no pressure to work late at the office on this day, and you know that you can stay on after dark because the trees are lit up as soon as night falls.

When you arrive, you take off your shoes, find yourself a square foot of mat, and start to relax. You smile at the latecomers who miss out on mat space and have to make a ground cover from the torn-off end of a cardboard box before taking off their shoes and sitting down near you. You know that even your tired workmates who nod off after ten minutes are enjoying はなみ in their own way.

In some places in Japan, はなみ can blossom into a week-long festival involving all sorts of things like folk-singing and dancing. But the cherry blossoms are the star attraction, and you sit and eat and drink and talk and experience and appreciate and... look, you really won't understand はなみ until you try it for yourself.

Names of places	
いとく	name of a supermarket
三かくビル	name of a skyscraper in しんじゅく area of 東京 (とうきょう)
だいまるデパート	name of a department store
マリオンえいがかん	name of a cinema
ミスタードーナツ	name of a doughnut chain store
みついビル	name of a skyscraper in しんじゅく area of 東京 (とうきょう)
みつこしデパート	name of a department store
ロッテリア	name of a hamburger chain store

三かくビルはみついビルの
まえにあります。

Expressions	
いいなあ	lucky you!
...はどこでしょうか。	can you tell me where ... is?
ごめん	sorry...
すみません	thank you
ざんねん	that's bad luck / that's too bad / how disappointing
ハーイ	hi!
まったく	really! You always say that!

食べものについて	
えきべん	べんとう purchased at stations
おにぎり	riceball/s
サンドイッチ	sandwich/es
たまご	egg/s
チキン	chicken
トリプル	triple (ice cream)
ダイエット中	on a diet
(お) ひるごはん (に)	(for) lunch
モカ	mocha flavour

単語	
おばさん	lady, woman
クラブの せんぱい	senior student in a club
こんばん	tonight
コンピューター	computer
(お)しろ	castle
バスてい	bus stop
バースデー	birthday

Adjectives	
いろいろ (な)	various
おそい	late
とおい	far
とくべつ (な)	special
べんり (な)	handy, convenient
ロマンティック (な)	romantic

例:
A すみませんが...えきはどこでしょうか。

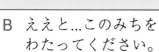

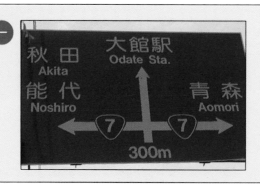

B ええと...このみちをまっすぐ行ってください。

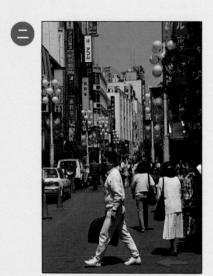

B ええと...このはしを
わたってください。

B ええと...このみちを
わたってください。

B ええと...そのかどを
左にまがってください

B ええと...つぎのかどを
右にまがってください。

Where is the station? Give directions using the examples as a guide.

一

二

三

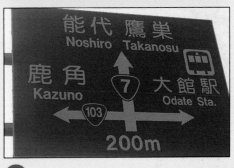

四

五

Now ask and give the right directions to the station according to each photo.

一

二

三

四

五

⊠⊠

A　このへんにバスていはありますか。
B　バスていですか。ロッテリアのまえに
　　ありますよ。

バスてい

ロッテリア

一　ポスト

えき

二　こうしゅうでんわ

えき

三　タクシーのりば

こうえん

四　こうしゅうでんわ

えいがかん

五　バスてい

えき

六　タクシーのりば

こうえん

Using the examples as a guide, ask and explain where things are around here.

例:
A　このへんにポストはありますか。
B　ポストですか。えきのまえにありますよ。

一 ゆうびんきょく

二 小学校

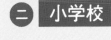

三 こうえん

四 えき

Ask and explain where the taxi stand is, using the example as a guide.

例：
A このへんにタクシーのりばはありますか。
B はい、ありますよ。このみちをまっすぐ行ってください。
　そうすると、ゆうびんきょくがあります。
　タクシーのりばはゆうびんきょくのまえにあります。

Look at the map and, using the examples as a guide,
explain how to get to the various places.

例:
A このへんにゆうびんきょくはありますか。
B ええと...つぎのかどを右にまがってください。
　　そうすると、ゆうびんきょくは左がわにあります。

例:
A このへんにぎんこうはありますか。
B ぎんこうですか。ええと...このはしをわたって、
　　二つめのかどを右にまがってください。ぎんこうは
　　左がわにあります。

⊠⊠ 弘前 (ひろさき) は青森県 (あおもりけん) にあります。大館 (おおだて) から
あまりとおくないです。弘前 (ひろさき) にゆうめいな
弘前城 (ひろさきじょう) があります。大学もあります。はるよく
弘前城 (ひろさきじょう) へはなみに行きます。

ぼくはゆたかです。せんしゅうの
日よう日にガールフレンドのみわちゃん
といっしょに弘前 (ひろさき) に行きました。とても
いいてんきでした。

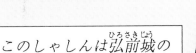

きれいなさくら!

岩木山 Iwakisan
弘前城 Hirosaki Castle
亀甲門 Kamenokomon
鯵ヶ沢 Ajigasawa

ええと、弘前城 (ひろさきじょう) はこのみちをまっすぐ
行って... 右にまがって...

このしゃしんは弘前城 (ひろさきじょう) の
もんのまえです。

弘前公園案内図

すみません、チケットうりばは
どこでしょうか。

ここですよ。このみちをまっすぐ
行ってください。そうすると、
右がわにありますよ。

にゅうじょうけんを
二まいください。

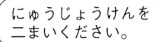

大人300円 小人100円
大人30 小人10

600円です。

6

はしをわたって、しろに行きました。

7

そして、しゃしんを
とりました。

こうえんでみんなははなみをしていました。
おべんとうを食べていました。

わたし、アイスクリーム食べたい。

すみません! このへんにアイスクリーム
スタンドはありますか。

あのかどを左にまがって、
右がわにありますよ。

8

アイスクリームを二つください。

9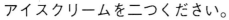

10

あっ、ようこさん、さとしくん、
こんにちは。げんき?

ぼくたちはゆっくりさんぽを
しました。ともだちのようこさんと
さとしくんにあいました。

あっ、ゆたかくん、見て。ボート！
たのしそう！のりたいね！

オッケー！

きもちいい！

それから、はなのトンネルに
行きました。とてもきれいでした。

おなかペコペコ！

単語	
はなみ	cherry blossom viewing
青森県 (あおもりけん)	Aomori Prefecture
弘前城 (ひろさきじょう)	Hirosaki Castle
さくら	cherry blossoms
もん	gate
チケットうりば	ticket box
にゅうじょうけん	admission ticket
〜まい	counter for thin, flat objects
アイスクリームスタンド	ice-cream stand
ゆっくり	slowly, leisurely
のりたい	want to ride in
きもちいい	this is great!
トンネル	tunnel
おなかペコペコ	I'm starving!
でぐち	exit
フランク	frankfurt
ジャンボポテト	baked potato

こうえんのでぐちのそばのみせで、
フランクとジャンボポテトを食べました。
でも、まずかった！

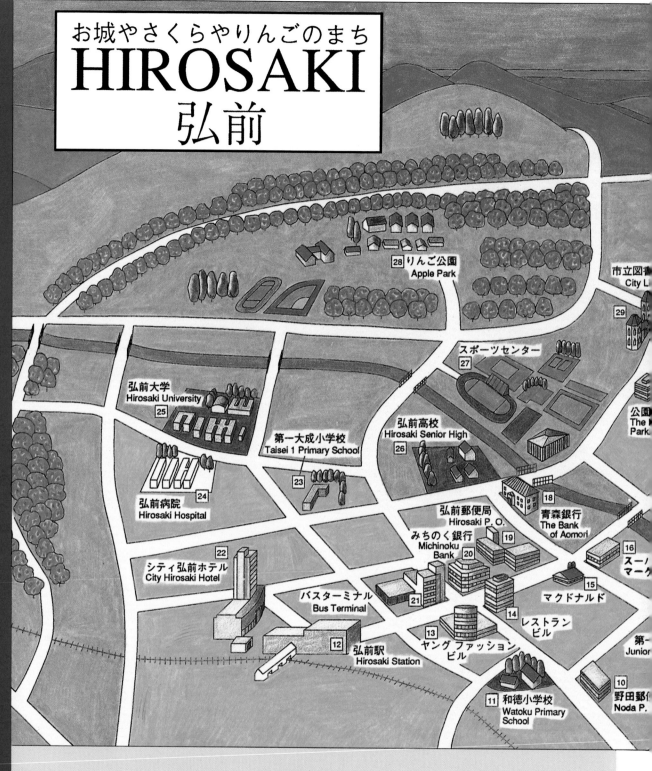

お城やさくらやりんごのまち
HIROSAKI
弘前

28 りんご公園
Apple Park

市立図書
City Li

29

スポーツセンター
27

弘前大学
Hirosaki University
25

第一大成小学校
Taisei 1 Primary School
23

弘前高校
Hirosaki Senior High
26

公園
The Park

弘前病院
Hirosaki Hospital
24

弘前郵便局
Hirosaki P. O.

青森銀行
The Bank
of Aomori
18

みちのく銀行
Michinoku
Bank
20

19

16

スー
マー

シティ弘前ホテル
City Hirosaki Hotel
22

バスターミナル
Bus Terminal

21

マクドナルド

15

14 レストラン
ビル

第一
Junior

12 弘前駅
Hirosaki Station

13 ヤング ファッション
ビル

11 和徳小学校
Watoku Primary
School

10
野田郵便
Noda P.

― すみませんが...弘前城<ruby>ひろさきじょう</ruby>はどこでしょうか。

You have arrived at Hirosaki Station and picked up the map from
the Information Centre. Your partner will take the role of a student
from Hirosaki and tell you how to get to places of interest.

You will of course want to go to the castle, to Toshogu Shrine,
to the Apple Park...

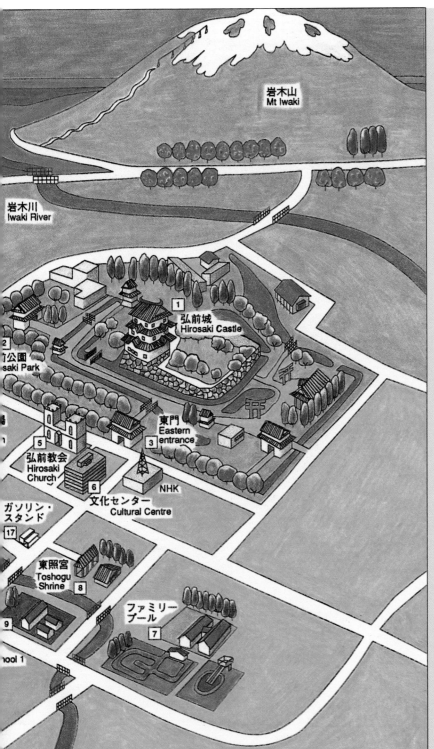

岩木山
Mt Iwaki

岩木川
Iwaki River

弘前城
Hirosaki Castle

弘前公園
...saki Park

東門
Eastern
entrance

弘前教会
Hirosaki
Church

NHK

文化センター
Cultural Centre

ガソリン・
スタンド

東照宮
Toshogu
Shrine

ファミリー
プール

...hool 1

二　このへんにガソリン スタンドは ありますか。

While eating lunch at マクドナルド you ask the person at your table (again a role played by your partner) if there are certain things in the area. You might like to find out if there's a supermarket, a bank, a sports centre, a library, a post office, a bus station...

Finding your way around

Question: Who are the best readers of ローマじ in all of Japan?

Answer: The people who deliver the mail!

Why? Because they are the ones who have to read the addresses on envelopes coming to Japan from all over the world. In fact, they are easily the best at it because not many Japanese people can read ローマじ at all.

Imagine those post-persons handling all the letters from Kimono students writing to Simone:

3-21, 1-chome, Yukinoshita
Kamakura-shi, Kanagawa-ken.

Ken means prefecture, *shi* is the city, *Yukinoshita* is the area, *chome* is the city block, 3 the lot number and 21 the house number.

So the mail people practise their ローマじ and the letters find their way to the right address. But for visitors to Japan, finding an address can be quite a challenge. For a start, there is no guarantee that the houses in a given street will be numbered in sequence. House number 3, for example, may have that number because it was the third house built in the street!

So, you can't rely on numbers, and it's no use pinning all your hopes on street signs either: in most Japanese cities it is only the main streets that are sign-posted. So how do you find your way around? By referring to landmarks, such as prominent buildings or other features of a particular area. Look at the business card above for a そば restaurant in しんばし, for example.

Do you see? No street names, no numbers, just the location of well-known local buildings such as a bank and a *pachinko* parlour. You have to get used to little maps like this in Japan. There are even some デパート that leave a space on their order forms for you to sketch a map so that their delivery people can find their way to your place.

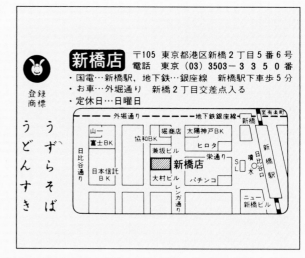

Asking and giving directions is a skill which most がいじん do not have, and that is why some Japanese taxi drivers don't like picking up foreign passengers. They just get into the back seat, give an address and expect to be taken there. Unless it's a really well-known place, what the driver needs is some helpful directions: it's near the park, turn left, drive until you reach the new hotel, turn right... And don't be surprised if the taxi driver drops you in the neighbourhood of the address you want and expects you to find the rest of your way there.

The Japanese might not have much in the way of street numbers and signs, but they do have こうばん - police boxes. These mini police stations are to be found on neighbourhood corners all over Japanese cities. Inside there is a grid with all the buildings and houses in that particular district marked on it. こうばん are staffed by local neighbourhood police officers who know everyone in that area and who will be able to tell you how to find their place. These police officers get to know the locals when they stroll around, patrolling their district. For this reason they are known as おまわりさん, Mr (or Ms) Walkaround.

But don't think the おまわりさん takes all the worry out of directions. When you ask at the こうばん, you still have to be able to understand when you are told where to go!

左

Meaning: *left*

Readings
ひだり

左・ひだり

 左 左

右

Meaning: *right*

Readings
みぎ

右・みぎ

 右 右

学

Meaning: *learning*

Readings

がく

学校・がっこう
大学・だいがく

 学 学

校

Meaning: *place of learning*

Readings

こう

学校・がっこう
小学校・しょうがっこう
中学校・ちゅうがっこう

 校 校

一 Telling where things are

To find out if there is a particular thing like a post-box around where you are, you ask

このへんにポストはありますか。
Is there a post-box around here?

There are various ways to answer this. A common way of starting is to confirm.

e.g. ポストですか。　ええと...
A post box...?　　Umm...

You confirm to give yourself extra time to think. ええと... does this too.

You then might give directions to a landmark.

このみちをまっすぐ行ってください。
そうすると、ゆうびんきょくが
あります。
Go straight along this street. Then you'll see a post office.

Particle が always follows this landmark.

Finally you explain the location of the object in terms of the landmark.

ポストはゆうびんきょくのまえに
あります。
The post-box is in front of the post office.

ポストはゆうびんきょくの
まえにあります。

二 Particles and directions

When you are giving directions, use の to describe a particular corner.

e.g. 本やのかど
the corner where the bookshop is
二つめのかど
the second corner
しんごうのかど
the corner that has traffic lights

Use を when directing someone to *go around*, *along*, or *across* something.

e.g. つぎのかどをまがってください。
Turn (at) the next corner.
はしをわたってください。
Cross the bridge.
このみちをまっすぐ行って
ください。
Go straight along this street.

Use に after the direction when telling someone to turn left or right.

e.g. しんごうのかどを右にまがって
ください。
Turn right at the corner that has traffic lights.
三つめのかどを左にまがって
ください。
Turn left at the third corner.

三 て form and directions

When you are giving directions, you often suggest a series of actions (e.g. going, turning, crossing). To link these different actions in one sentence, use the て form to get the verb meaning, plus *and*.

e.g. このみちをわたって、つぎのかどを
左にまがってください。
Cross this street and turn left at the next corner.
このみちをまっすぐ行って、
ぎんこうのかどを右にまがって
ください。
Go straight along this street and turn right at the corner where the bank is.

Directions

このへんに	around here, in this vicinity
左(ひだり)	left
左がわ	left-hand side
右 (みぎ)	right
右がわ	right-hand side
まっすぐ	straight
まがる (まがります)	to turn
わたる (わたります)	to cross

Expressions

そうすると...	after that, then...
このみちをまっすぐ行ってください	go straight along this street
このはしをわたってください	cross this bridge
二つめのかどを右にまがってください	turn right at the second corner
つぎのかどを左にまがってください	turn left at the next corner

みせのかど

Places

かど	corner
こうしゅうでんわ	public phone
ガソリンスタンド	petrol station
ぎんこう	bank
しんごう	traffic lights
タクシーのりば	taxi stand
はし	bridge
びょういん	hospital
ポスト	post box
みち	street, road
ゆうびんきょく	post office

しんごうのかど

カメラやのかど

Counters

～まい	for counting flat, thin objects, e.g. tickets, sheets of paper, records, shirts
一つめの...	the first...
二つめの...	the second... etc.

やすいね。この
オレンジの...

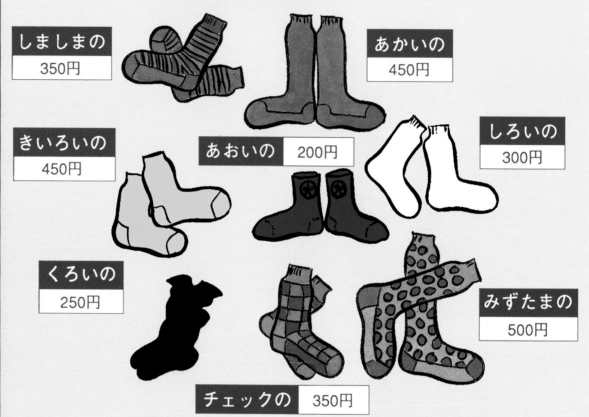

しましまの
350円

あかいの
450円

きいろいの
450円

あおいの　200円

しろいの
300円

くろいの
250円

みずたまの
500円

チェックの　350円

What do you think of these socks?
Make your comments using the examples
as a guide.

Can you find the design you want?
Using the examples as a guide, ask both
your friend and the salesperson.

例:

A　このしましまのはどう?
B　うん、いいね。
　　or
　　ううん、ちょっと...

例:

A　しましまの、ある?
B　うん、ここにある。
　　or
　　ううん、ない。

A　このしましまのはどうですか。
B　ええ、いいですね。
　　or
　　それはちょっと...

A　しましまのはありますか。
B　ええ、ここにあります。
　　or
　　いいえ、ありません。

土よう日のごご

1

どこ行くの？　ジャスコ。

2

ジャスコで何するの？

三かいのゲームセンターであそぶんだ。

いっしょに行ってもいい？

オッケー。

3

何買うの？

しょうじくんのバースデープレゼント。

4

このシャツ、どう？

うん、まあまあね。

5

見て、見て。このトレーナーいいね。

いいいろね。

このあかいのはどう？

いいけど...

このえい語わかる？

ううん。ぜんぜん...。

このあおいのはどう？

7

ううん、ちょっと...。みどりのある？

6

このしろいのは？

ちょっと小さいかな。

すみません。あのオレンジいろの
パーカを見せてください。

9

8

はい、あれはMサイズ
ですが...Lサイズと
ＬＬサイズもあります。

じゃ、ＬＬサイズのをください。

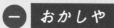
一 おかしや

二 ともだちのうち

三 川

四 学校

五 びょういん

六 としょかん

Talk about where you are going, using the examples as a guide.

例:
A どこ行くの?
B おかしや行くの。
A おかしや?
B うん。

A どこ行くの?
B おかしや。
A おかしや?
B うん。

一 ビデオ見る

二 でかける

三 ねる

四 てがみかく

五 まんがよむ

六 ＣＤきく

七 プラモデルつくる

八 いぬあらう

九 トランプする

Talk about what you are going to do tonight,
using the examples as a guide for your conversation.

 例:
A こんばん何するの?
B ビデオ見るの。
A ふうん。

 例:
A こんばん何するの?
B ビデオ見るんだ。
A ふうん。

例:
A こんばん何をしますか。
B ビデオを見ます。
A そうですか。

⊗⊗

一

かがくのしゅくだい
すうがくのしゅくだい
れきしのしゅくだい

二

きょうしつのそうじ
へやのそうじ
うちのそうじ

Using the examples as a guide, talk about what you will do today. The expressions in the boxes may be helpful.

例:

A　きょう何するの?
B　かがくのしゅくだいするの。
A　しゅくだい? たいへんね!

A　きょう何するの?
B　かがくのしゅくだいするんだ。
A　しゅくだい? たいへんだね!

A　きょう何をしますか。
B　かがくのしゅくだいをします。
A　しゅくだいですか。たいへんですね。

 一

二

三

 四

五

六

してる	食べてる	のんでる
よんでる	買ってる	まってる

Using the examples as a guide, talk about what these people are doing. The verbs given in the box may be helpful.

例:

A　いま何してるの?
B　ともだちまってるの。
　　or
　　ううん、べつに...

A　いま何してるの?
B　ともだちまってるんだ。
　　or
　　ううん、べつに...

Make up a conversation with a partner about your plans for tonight. Decide who will be A and who will be B. Take care to use the appropriate speech for males and females.

A	オス! おはよう! こんにちは!	何してるの?	

B	本 ざっし まんが	よんでるの よんでるんだ

A	どんな	本 ざっし まんが	すき?

B	くるま スポーツ ポップミュージック	の	本。 ざっし。 まんが。

A	よくよむ?

B	ううん、	ときどき。 たまに。

A	テレビは?

B	うん、すき。

A	ぼくも。 わたしも。	こんばん	ウィンブルドンのテニス マドンナのコンサート F-1 (Formula one) レース	見る?

B	うん、見る、見る。	[A]さん [A]くん	も見る?

A	ううん、見たいけど...こんばん	でかけるの。 でかけるんだ。

B	どこ行くの?

A	おばあさんのうち行くの。 おばあさんのうち。 ケンとデートするの。 アンとデートするんだ。 レストラン行くの。 レストラン。

B	かわいそう! いいね!

火

Meaning: *fire*

Readings
ひ
か

火・ひ

火曜日・かようび

水

Meaning: *water*

Readings
みず
すい

水・みず

水曜日・すいようび

金

Meaning: *gold, metal*

Readings
かね
きん

お金・おかね

金曜日・きんようび

木

Meaning: *tree, wood*

Readings
き
もく

木・き

木曜日・もくようび

Opposite is a department store guide which tells you what is on each floor.

1 You are finding out where various things are by asking at the information desk. Your partner will play the role of the assistant. Some sample dialogues have been given below.

When you ask at the information desk, the assistant will use some very polite words. For example, でございます is used instead of です and ございます is used in place of あります. You won't need to use these words very much but it's important to understand them.

A ベルトうりばは何かいでしょうか。
B 四かいでございます。

A 四かいにトイレはありますか。
B はい、ございます。

A 五かいにトイレはありますか。
B いいえ、四かいにございます。

2 At the entrance to the store you are looking at the guide with your friend. With your partner, practise asking and telling on what floors various things are. Below are some sample dialogues to get you started.

A ベルトうりばは何かいかな？
B ああ、四かいよ。

A ベルトうりばは何かいかな？
B ああ、四かいだよ。

A 四かいにトイレある？
B うん、あるよ。
A 五かいにトイレある？
B ううん、四かい。

単語
…うりば …sales area
トイレ toilet

3 When you meet your friend in the lift, you will want to know where they are going and what they plan to buy. Practise this conversation with your partner. Some sample dialogues have been given below.

A 何かい行くの？
B 四かい行くの。
A 何買うの？
B ジーンズ買うの。
A ふうん。

A 何かい行くの？
B 四かい。
A 何買うの？
B ジーンズ買うんだ。
A ふうん。

八かい		
美術	びじゅつ	art and craft
人形	にんぎょう	dolls
時計	とけい	watches
料理	りょうり	food
七かい		
書籍	しょせき	publications
電気器具	でんききぐ	electrical goods
雑誌	ざっし	magazines
洗濯機	せんたくき	washing machines
冷蔵庫	れいぞうこ	refrigerators
六かい		
子供服	こどもふく	children's wear
B1		
食品	しょくひん	foodstuffs
菓子	かし	confectionery
茶	ちゃ	green tea
紅茶	こうちゃ	tea
弁当	べんとう	prepared lunches
酒	さけ	rice wine
鮮魚	せんぎょ	fresh fish
肉	にく	meat
地下鉄	ちかてつ	underground railway
B2		
駐車場	ちゅうしゃじょう	car park

Tamamiya

R	グリーンハウス ペットのフロア	ペットコーナー ゲームコーナー	ジュース、アイスクリーム スタンド		
8	レストラン 美術のフロア	ギャラリー	きもの 人形 時計	レストラン てんぷら　　　　すし そば　うどん フランス料理 イタリア料理	
7	オーディオサウンド 書籍、 電気器具のフロア	ミュージックサロン CD カセット ビデオテープ	本、雑誌 コンピューター カメラ	電気器具 洗濯機　冷蔵庫 テレビ　ラジカセ ビデオデッキ	
6	子供服　スポーツ ステーショナリー のフロア	スポーツ スポーツウエア サイクリング ジョギング シェイプアップ	ゴルフショップ テニスショップ	ステーショナリー　こども ペン、コイン　　　ベビーウエア アルバム　　　　　ティーンズ カード ラッピング	
5	インテリア ホームリビングのフロア	カーテン カーペット ランプ	ルームアクセサリー　エプロン 　　　　　　　　　テーブルクロス	バストイレタリー スリッパ ラ　　ターブル	
4	メンズのフロア	セーター シャツ	ジャケット パンツ	ネクタイ ベルト	メンズカジュアル　スーツ ジーンズ　　　　　コート	
3	レディスのフロア	ニット　セーター ブラウス パンツ	インターナショナル ブティック フォーマル	ドレス コート	ライラックプラザ (大きいサイズ)スカート	
2	ヤングカジュアル のフロア	すずらんプラザ (小さいサイズ) ヤングフォーマル	ベネトン T・シャツ ジャケット	ジーンズ	ゴルフファッション トレンディ	
1	アクセサリー のフロア	ハンドバッグギャラリー フラワーブティック ギフトカード	ハンカチ スカーフ ベルト ソックス ストッキング	くつ シューズギャラリー	
B1	食品のフロア	菓子 茶 コーヒー 紅茶 トワイニング フォートナムメイソン	デザート　ケーキ サンドイッチスタジオ 弁当 　　　酒 　　　ワイン 　　　ビール	鮮魚　肉　ハム やさい 地下鉄のりば	 ティアモ
B²	駐車場				

Can you work out what these signs mean? After you have worked
out as much as you can, use the sample dialogue below to check
if your friend knows as much as you.

A　このサイン、わかる?
B　うん、すこし。
　　or
　　うん、だいたい。
　　or
　　ううん、ぜんぜん。

一

二

三

四

五

六

単語	
すこし	a bit
だいたい	generally, mostly

The authors
Kimono
CIS Educational

Dear Sir/Madam,

You haven't actually met me. I'm Simone - you know, the one who wrote those letters from Japan back to my classmates. I knew that you were going to put some of my letters in your books because the school asked me if it would be all right, but it was great to actually see them when I got back home. I still read over them and they remind me of what it was like when I was there.

But I'm back now, and I have to settle down and get used to home again. It's a lot harder than I thought it would be. You might find this hard to understand, but I don't feel 'different' any more. I don't sort of stand out like I did in Japan. I thought I would like just being one of the crowd again, and I do, but sometimes I miss being, I don't know, special, I suppose.

One thing I know is that I have to stop bowing. I didn't realise I was so much into the habit, but I'm bowing all over the place to all sorts of people. They don't know what to make of it, and sometimes I try and change a bow into just leaning over to pick something up. And the other thing is I keep saying そう? and putting ね at the end of everything I say. These little words have become so much a part of the way I speak, it's hard to realise that people here have never heard them before. And that reminds me - everyone says that my accent is funny when I'm speaking English. They just say it doesn't sound natural or something. I'm sure it won't be long before I get my old accent back.

One of the best things about being back is being able to read all the signs. I drove my family mad on the way home from the airport, reading out exciting things like 'Next exit 500 metres' and all the advertisements I could see. And it's just sheer luxury being able to watch TV without having to concentrate really hard to understand what they are saying. I didn't realise how much effort I was putting into understanding things in Japan, even after all those months.

But the real reason I'm writing to you is to tell you about a problem I am having at school. It has to do with Japanese language, and I think that if you are going to write Kimono 3, the students should know about it.

The thing is, I keep clashing with my Japanese teacher. Every time I see her, I start talking to her in 日本語, and every time she ends up looking really uncomfortable and saying that I'm using らんぼうなことば. In other words, she is telling me my speech is rough. I found it hard to accept at first because that was the way I always spoke to my friends and to the family I was staying with in Japan.

They always used to say 日本語がじょうずだね. I'll give you an example. The other day I saw my teacher and said, せんせい、こんばんテレビ見る? Just trying to be friendly, show a bit of interest. Well, she just looked at me and said, せんせい、こんばんテレビを見ますか. That was the way she wanted me to say it. I mean, after all that time in Japan, I thought the big advantage would be not having my Japanese corrected. I thought I would probably know more than my teacher. But she started explaining to me about the difference between polite speech and plain speech.

She said it was fine to drop です／ます form and the particles when I was with my friends but I shouldn't use plain speech when speaking with people like teachers and other adults who are not in the family or really close friends. Now I understand what my teacher in Japan once tried to explain to me in 日本語. Now I'm actually a bit embarrassed about the way I must have sounded to some of the people I met over there.

Just when I thought I had the idea, my teacher came up to me at the lockers the other day and said, 何してるの? You know, plain speech. Well, I thought she must have changed her mind, she must have decided we were like friends. So I answered, ともだちまってるんだ. As soon as she started her frown, I knew I was in for another らんぼうなことば. She explained that it was all right for a teacher to use plain speech with a student, but students must always use polite speech with teachers. I just blush now to think of the mistakes I must have made with my teachers in Japan.

All my friends are calling me Rambo now. My teacher says it suits me. You know - rough speech, talking like a boy and all that. But I am learning. The other morning I saw her near the library. I just automatically said オス! then, hoping she hadn't heard that, I blurted out おはよう. Then just before the dreaded frown, I managed to get in ございます. She just smiled and sort of made a tick in the air.

I thought people studying your book should know about this so that they won't make the mistakes I made. I hope you explain it to them properly. All the best with Kimono 3 (if there is one).

Yours sincerely,
Simone
シモーン

P.S. I know you won't use this but I've enclosed a picture of me that someone stuck up on my locker.

日本語ノート

一 Even more about の

You can use の to mean *one* in expressions like *the red one*, *the 200円 one*...

e.g. そのシャツいいね。きいろいのはどう？

These shirts are good, aren't they? What do you think of the yellow one?

3000円のをください。
I'll have the 3000-yen one.

二 Plain speech form of verbs

Compare these two sentences:

こんばんテレビ見る？
こんばんテレビを見ますか。

They both ask if you are going to watch TV tonight. The first sentence is in *plain* speech while the second one asks in *polite* speech.

When you speak informally with your family and friends, you do not need to use verbs in their 〜ます endings. You can use the plain form of the verb. This form is also called the *dictionary form* as verbs are listed in the dictionary in plain form.

How you make the plain form depends on what kind of verb you are dealing with. For *weak* verbs, you simply drop 〜ます and add る.

e.g. 食べます　食べる
見ます　　見る
おきます　おきる

When you change *strong* verbs into plain form, you drop 〜ます and change the final 'i' sound to 'u'.

e.g. まがります　まがる　らりるれろ
よみます　　よむ　　まみむめも
あらいます　あらう　あいうえお
まちます　　まつ　　たちつてと

Look at the corresponding lines from the ひらがな table next to each example and you can see more clearly how these *strong* verbs change.

Within the *irregular* group of verbs, 行きます and あります change in the same way as *strong* verbs. Note carefully that します changes to する and きます in the plain form is くる.

〜ます form	plain form
weak verbs	
あけます	あける
います	いる
しめます	しめる
食べます	食べる
でかけます	でかける
できます	できる
ねます	ねる
見ます	見る
strong verbs	
つくります	つくる
まがります	まがる
わかります	わかる
わたります	わたる
あらいます	あらう
買います	買う
つかいます	つかう
たちます	たつ
まちます	まつ
かきます	かく
храききます	きく
ひきます	ひく
およぎます	およぐ
あそびます	あそぶ
のみます	のむ
よみます	よむ
かします	かす
はなします	はなす
irregular verbs	
あります	ある
行きます	行く
きます	くる
します	する

第四課
● 五十八

いま、ぼくねてるんだ。

何してるの？　すみません。

三　Asking questions in plain form

a　With a question word

When you ask a question in plain speech and use a question word like どこ, いつ, 何 etc., の is used at the end of the sentence.

e.g. どこ行くの？
Where are you going?

何買うの？
What are you going to buy?

Male and female speakers respond differently to questions that use の. Look at these different answers to the same question.

きょう何するの？
What are you doing today?

 でかけるの。

 でかけるんだ。
I'm going out.

行く is a common exception to this for male speakers. A male, when asked where he is going, will probably respond with just the place.

e.g. どこ行くの？
Where are you going?

ともだちのうち。
To my friend's place.

b　Without a question word

If there is no question word used, then の is not usually used in either the question or the answer.

e.g. こんばんテレビ見る？
Are you going to watch TV tonight?

うん、見る。
Yeah.

このサインわかる？
Do you understand this sign?

うん、わかる。
Yeah, I do.

The verbs 行く and する often use の in questions with no question words.

e.g. まち行くの？
Are you going to town?

よくするの？
Do you play often?

It is impossible to give hard and fast rules for plain speech because it is the language of informal situations. The speech patterns given here are common ones in Japanese, but don't be surprised if you hear people — both male and female — using different patterns.

四　〜て(い)ます in plain form

The plain form of verbs in the 〜ています form is 〜ている. In plain speech, this is shortened to 〜てる.

The same rules for the use of の and male and female speech apply when using this form.

e.g. いま何してるの？
What are you doing?

 ともだちまってるの。

 ともだちまってるんだ。
I'm waiting for my friend.

Expressions

ある	there is
ない	there isn't
かわいそう	poor you!
がっかりしちゃう	Oh no!! I'm so disappointed! What a blow!
サンキュー	thank you
しんじられない	I don't believe this...
ぜんぜん	not at all
たいへん	how awful!
ちょっと	it's a bit...
べつに	nothing in particular, nothing much
まあまあ	so-so
わかる?	do you understand?

トランプしてるんだ。

単語

...けど	but...
サイズ	size
しましま(の)	striped
(お)そうじ	cleaning
そうじする	to do the cleaning
ジャスコ	name of a department store
チェック(の)	checked
トランプ	playing cards
トランプする	to play cards
プラモデル	plastic model
みずたま(の)	spotted

Counting floors

何かい	なんかい	what floor?
ちかにかい		second floor basement
ちかいっかい		basement
一かい	いっかい	first floor, ground floor
二かい	にかい	second floor
三かい	さんかい	third floor
四かい	よんかい	fourth floor
五かい	ごかい	fifth floor
六かい	ろっかい	sixth floor
七かい	ななかい	seventh floor
八かい	はちかい	eighth floor
九かい	きゅうかい	ninth floor
十かい	じゅっかい	tenth floor
おくじょう		rooftop

くみこさんのおにいさんのかぞくについて

これはあにのみせで、なまえは
大吉だ。

あにはけっこんしている。

あにとともこさんとこどもの
たけしの三人かぞくだ。

おいのたけしは六さいで、
とてもかわいい。

みせはごご五時から
十一時までだが、あには三時はんから
じゅんびする。ばんごはんはいつも
四時はんに食べる。

このやきとり
おいしそう！

あにはあさねぼうして十時に

ぼく六さい！

おきる。でも、たけしの
ようちえんはあさ九時にはじまる。
だから、ともこさんは六時はんにおきて、
あさごはんとたけしのおべんとうをつくる。
ともこさんは何時間ねられるかな？かわいそう！
みせのやすみはまいしゅう日よう日だ。時々
あにのかぞくはいっしょにでかける。

ああ、いそがしい！

はい、どうぞ。

ミーティングは何時から何時まで?

いいましょう 一

一　ぎんこう　9.00 -15.00

二　ゆうびんきょく
9.00 - 5.00

三　ビデオ ショップ
11.00am - 10.00pm

四　としょかん
10.00 - 4.30

五　デパート
10.00 -6.00

六　プール ・ 7.00 - 9.30

Using the examples as a guide, talk about the
opening and closing times of these places.

例:
A　ぎんこうは何時から?
B　九時からよ。
A　何時まで?
B　三時までよ。

例:
A　ぎんこうは何時から?
B　九時からだよ。
A　何時まで?
B　三時までだよ。

A　ぎんこうは何時からですか。
B　九時からですよ。
A　何時までですか。
B　三時までですよ。

例:
A　ぎんこうは何時から
何時まで?
B　九時から三時までよ。

A　ぎんこうは何時から
何時まで?
B　九時から三時までだよ。

A　ぎんこうは何時から
何時までですか。
B　九時から三時までですよ。

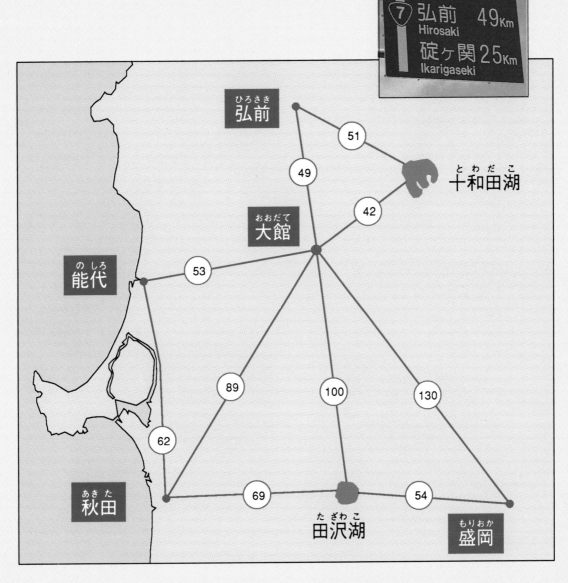

Talk about the distances between the cities
on the map, using the examples as a guide.

 例:
A 大館から弘前まで何キロ?
B 49キロよ。

A 大館から弘前まで何キロ?
B 49キロだよ。

A 大館から弘前まで何キロ
ですか。
B 49キロですよ。

 例:
A 弘前から十和田湖まで何キロ?
B 51キロよ。

A 弘前から十和田湖まで何キロ?
B 51キロだよ。

A 弘前から十和田湖まで
何キロですか。
B 51キロですよ。

⊠⊠

くみこさんのおねえさんのみほさんについて

わたしのあねのみほははたちで、弘前大学に
かよっている。大学はたいてい、八時はんに
はじまって、二時はんにおわる。まい日
六時はんにおきて、七時にうちをでる。きしゃと
バスで大学に行く。うちから大学まで一時間はん
ぐらいかかる。

1

木よう日から日よう日まで
ミスタードーナツでバイトをしている。
時々大学をサボってアルバイトをする。
じきゅうは650円でしょくじつきだ。
ドーナツを食べてもいい。いいバイトだ。
あねはバイトのお金をつかって、すてきな
ようふくが買える。うらやましい。

> おそうじ、きらい。

2

> いやだねえ。

> ありがとうございました。またどうぞ。

3

4

5

> ハニーディップが二つ、カスタードクリームが三つ、
> それから、チョコドーナツが五つ...ええと、いくらかな。

> ああ！ おねえちゃん、
> 大学サボってる！

> ちがうよ。きょうは
> じゅぎょうないの！

> ほんと？

6

> ほんと！

単語

かよう	to commute, to go
(じゅぎょう)をサボる	to skip (classes)
買える	can buy, to be able to buy
ハニーディップ	honey-dipped doughnuts
カスタードクリーム	custard-filled doughnuts
ない	there isn't

一

学校

十五分

二

十和田湖

一時間はん

まち

十分

三

四

広島えき

二十五分

五

銀座

三十分

六

東京

二時間はん

七

ともだちのうち

一時間

How do you get to various places?
Find out, using the examples as a guide.

Using the examples as a guide, find
out how long it takes to get to places.

 例:
A 学校までどうやって行くの?
B じてんしゃで行くの。

 A 学校までどうやって行くの?
B じてんしゃで行くんだ。

A 学校までどうやって行きますか。
B じてんしゃで行きます。

 例:
A どのぐらいかかるの?
B 十五分ぐらい。

A どのぐらいかかりますか。
B 十五分ぐらい
かかりますよ。

The following dialogue is about plans for the weekend.
Make up a conversation with a partner.
Decide who will be A and who will be B.

A	しゅうまつ何するの?		
B	山	行くの。 行くんだ。	
A	へえ?	ハイキング スキー 山のぼり	するの?
B	ううん。	フィッシング じょうば	するの。 するんだ。
A	ああ、そう。いいね。どうやって行くの?		
B	くるま きしゃ バス	で	行くの。 行くんだ。
A	山までどのぐらいかかるの?		
B	そうねえ。	三時間はんぐらい。 四時間はんぐらい。 五時間ぐらい。	
A	へえ?! 山まで何キロ?		
B	ええと...	250キロ 350キロ 450キロ	よ。 だよ。
A	だれと行くの?		
B	かぞく 学校のともだち ボーイフレンド ガールフレンド	と	行くの。 行くんだ。
A	たのしそう! おもしろそう! うらやましい!	わたしもいっしょに行きたい!	
B	だめ! いいよ。		

ともだちとともだちとともだちとともだちと

時

Meaning: *time, hour*

Readings
とき
じ

時々・ときどき

何時・なんじ
四時・よじ

   時 時

間

Meaning: *an interval, between*

Readings
あいだ
かん

小学校と大学の間・しょうがっこうと
だいがくのあいだ

時間・じかん
一時間・いちじかん

 間 間

分

Meaning: *minute(s)*

Readings

ふん／ぷん

四分・よんぷん
五分・ごふん
十分・じゅっぷん, じっぷん

 分 分

々

Meaning: *repeat symbol for kanji*

Readings

時々・ときどき
人々・ひとびと

   々 々

⊠⊠

わたし、はぎわらきょうこ。あたらしいコーヒーの
キャンペーンガールよ。このバイトのじきゅうは1500円。
パーカももらえるの。いいバイトよ。でも、あさ七時から
ごご六時まで。ちょっとたいへん。

1

2

わたしのなまえはほしのちか。パンやのてんいんの
アルバイトしてるの。じきゅうは550円でしょくじつき。
土よう日と日よう日の十時から三時までバイトするの。

3

4

わたし、さいとうかおり。ディズニーランドで
バイトしてるの。じきゅうは650円で、
しょくじつき。いろいろな人にあえて、
がいこく人もたくさんくるの。時々えい語で
はなせるの。とてもたのしいバイトよ。

5

ぼく、いしかわようじ。弘前城のテレホン
カードうってるんだ。500円のと1000円のが
あるんだ。一まいどう？このバイトは
一時間1050円。でも、あめの日はさむくて
いやだよ。

6

ぼくたちのバイトはらくだよ。
こうえんでフィルムうってるんだ。
一時間800円で、日よう日の
十一時から六時まで。
あさねぼうできるんだ。

単語	
もらえる	can receive
あえる	can meet
はなせる	can speak
さむくて	cold and...

いってみましょう

一 バイト

You have decided that you really could do with some extra money and would like to apply for one of the part-time jobs advertised here. Your parents aren't very keen on your working as they think you should do more study. You will need to convince your mother or father (a role played by your partner) that the バイト is a good one. Some things that your parents will want to know about are: what kind of job it is, the hours that you will work, how much you'll be paid. You will want to be able to tell them about any other advantages that the job has.

ヘアカット モデル
募集(ぼしゅう)

15才から18才の男女
時給　￥700
毎週　火曜日：午後3時から 電話：3572−1209 ZIP　HAIR

募集(ぼしゅう)

キャンペーン ボーイ!!
キャンペーン ガール!!
新しいドリンクのキャンペーンを
して下さい。

時給・￥1600

8.00 am − 10.00 am
または
4.00 pm − 7.00 pm
☎：3343−9645
カスケード・ドリンク

単語			
募集 (ぼしゅう)	recruiting, hiring	15才	15さい
相談 (そうだん)	by arrangement	男女	males and females
食事付	しょくじつき	毎週	まいしゅう
新しい	あたらしい	火曜日	かようび
下さい	ください	午後	ごご
時給	じきゅう	電話	でんわ

ニ　テレビガイド

Your parents have decided that you and your brother or sister (a role played by your partner) are watching too much TV. They have told you both that on Saturday night you may watch two hours of television and that you have to agree about what you would like to see. Since your parents want to see your choices in advance, you need to be specific about the following points:

what sort of program it is (e.g. スポーツ, まんが, クイズ, えいが...);
which channel it is on; what time it starts and finishes.

Using the テレビガイド, choose the programs you would like to see and negotiate with your brother or sister to arrange your two hours of viewing.

土
Saturday

	1 NHK	4 日本テレビ	6 TBS テレビ	8 フジテレビ	10 テレビ朝日	
6	6.00 NHK 経済マガジン ＊レポート92 スーパーテク	6.00 ニュース・プラス1 ※今日のニュース ◆天気	6.00 料理 「オーストラリアの オージービーフ」 6.30 ※ニュース 6.55 ◆天気	6.00 ＊N FNN スーパータイム 6.30 スペシャル・ナイター 「ヤクルトX巨人」	6.00 ワールド・ビッグテニス 「レンドル X マッケンロー」 6.30 ザ・スクープ ウィークレポート	6
7	7.00 7時のニュース ※nc 桜井洋子 ◆天気 7.30 クイズ・百点満点 「海で遊ぶ」	7.00 サタデー スーパー・スペシャル ＊オールスター・ デビュー・ フェスティバル ＊アイドルタレントの コンテスト	7.00 まんが日本むかしばなし 「かぐやひめ」 7.30 クイズダービー 「ミュージカル大会」		7.00 バッグス・バニー 7.30 いつか行く旅 「ニュージーランド」	7
8	8.00 サスペンス・ドラマ アガサ・クリスティの 「ベールをかけた女」 9.30 北海道の旅	＊キャンペーンガールの インフォメーション ＊コマーシャルのスター 9.00 今夜のゴールデンドラマ 「もう一度ロマンス」	8.00 加トちゃんケンちゃん ごきげんテレビ ＊田中陽子 ＊おもしろい ビデオコーナー 9.00 クイズ・世界ふしぎ発見 「スペイン・ バルセロナ」	8.50 ※N FNN ◆天気 8.58 ハロー・ムービーズ! 「ニュー・ムービー インフォメーション」 9.00 土曜ゴールデン映画 「レイダース・ 失われたアーク」 ＊ハリソン・フォード	8.00 クイズ・ヒントでピント 8.30 時代劇スペシャル 「暴れん坊将軍」 9.26 ※ANN N & ◆あすの天気 9.30 土曜ワイド・ドラマ 「京都殺人事件」	8
9						9
10	10.00 ※N ◆天気 10.15 サタデースポーツ 「ハイライト」 プロ野球、大相撲 ウィンブルドンテニス 10.45	10.45 ※N ◆天気	10.00 ドラマチック22 「東京まゆつばCITY」	10.54 おいしいレストラン ガイド	10.30 ANN ナイトライン	10
11	ショータイム 「マドンナ onステージ」	11.00 オールナイト・スポーツ スペシャル 「インサイド・ザ・ PGA ツアー」		11.00 ヒットスタジオ・SUPER MTV ジャパン	11.00 ミュージック 「ストレンジャー」	11

天気	てんき		大会	たいかい	tournament
経済	けいざい	economics	世界ふしぎ発見	せかい ふしぎ はっけん	
北海道の旅	ほっかいどうの たび	travelling in Hokkaido			mysteries of the world
野球、	やきゅう		東京	とうきょう	
大相撲	おおずもう	sumo wrestling	ナイター		night baseball game
今日	きょう		ヤクルトX 巨人	きょじん	Yakult versus Giants
今夜	こんや	tonight	土曜	どよう	
もう一度	もういちど	one more time	映画	えいが	
料理	りょうり	cooking	いつか行く旅	いつか いく たび	a trip I'd like to do
むかしばなし		fairy tales	時代劇	じだいげき	period dramas

一 …から and …まで

The particle から means *from* and you can add it to a time or a place.

e.g. テレビのニュースは七時から
です。
The TV news is on from 7 o'clock.
ここからとおいですか。
Is it far from here?

から follows the time or place word.

Like から, まで is also a particle which can follow a time or a place. まで means *until*, *as far as* and sometimes it can mean simply *to*.

e.g. きょうあさねぼうして、十一時
までねました。
Today I slept in until 11 o'clock.
うちまでとおくないですよ。
It's not far to my house.

から and まで are often used together.

e.g. 学校は八時はんから三時はん
までだよ。
School is from 8.30 to 3.30.
ここからえきまでどのぐらい
かかりますか。
How long does it take to get to the station from here?

二 で meaning *and*

あにのなまえはニックです。
My brother's name is Nick.
十七さいです。
He's 17.

You can join these two sentences by changing です to で.

あにのなまえはニックで、
十七さいです。
My brother's name is Nick and he's 17.

This で is the て form of です and can be translated as *and* when it is used in this way.

三 More about plain speech

As you know, in plain speech です changes to だ. Male speakers often use だ while female speakers tend to drop it.

 きょうとしょかんは 九時までよ。

 きょうとしょかんは 九時までだよ。

The library's open till 9 o'clock today.

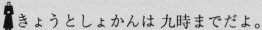 大館（おおだて）まで百キロよ。

大館（おおだて）まで百キロだよ。

It's 100 kilometres to Oodate.

四 Periods of time

間（かん）means *period* and when you add it to times, you are able to talk about how long something takes.

e.g. 学校までどのぐらいかかるの?
How long does it take to get to school?
一時間ぐらい。
About an hour.

Take care not to confuse 〜時, meaning *o'clock*, and 〜時間, meaning *hours*.

e.g. 九時にねました。
He went to bed at 9 o'clock.
九時間ねました。
He slept for nine hours.

To say that something takes an hour and a half, はん is added after 間.

e.g. きのう三時間はんべんきょう
しました。
Yesterday I studied for three and a half hours.

You do not have to use 間 when the time period is in minutes.

e.g. じてんしゃで十分かかります。
It takes ten minutes by bike.

五 Dropping particles

You have seen that the particles を, に and は are often dropped in plain speech. However, the particles と, meaning *with*, and で, meaning *by* or *at*, are not usually omitted.

e.g. 山まででんしゃで行くの。

We're going to the mountains *by* train.

単語	
いそがしい	busy
うらやましい	envious, jealous
から	from
きしゃ	train (for longer distances)
〜ぐらい	about, approximately (after amount)
テレホンカード	telephone card
だから	therefore
フィルム	film (for camera)
まで	until, up to, as far as, to
やすみ	holiday, rest
山のぼり	mountain climbing
ようちえん	kindergarten
ようふく	clothes
らく	easy, comfortable

Verbs	
あさねぼうする	to sleep in, to sleep late
うる	to sell
おわる	to end, to finish
かかる	to take time
じゅんびする	to prepare
でる	to leave
ねられる	can sleep
はじまる	to begin, to start

Expressions	
ちがう	no, (that's not the reason)
どうやって行く	how will you get there?
どのぐらい	how long?
ほんと	really

Periods of time

Hours		
何時間	なんじかん	how many hours?
一時間	いちじかん	one hour
二時間	にじかん	two hours
三時間	さんじかん	three hours
四時間	よじかん	four hours
五時間	ごじかん	five hours
十時間	じゅうじかん	ten hours
〜時間はん	〜じかんはん	...and a half hours

Minutes		
何分	なんぷん	how many minutes?
一分	いっぷん	one minute
二分	にふん	two minutes
三分	さんぷん	three minutes
四分	よんぷん	four minutes
五分	ごふん	five minutes
六分	ろっぷん	six minutes
七分	ななふん	seven minutes
八分	はっぷん	eight minutes
九分	きゅうふん	nine minutes
十分	じゅっぷん	ten minutes
十五分	じゅうごふん	fifteen minutes
二十分	にじゅっぷん	twenty minutes

バイトについて	
アルバイト／バイト	part-time job
お金 (おかね)	money
キャンペーンガール	campaign girl
キャンペーンボーイ	campaign boy
しょくじつき	meals provided
じきゅう	hourly rate
てんいん	shop assistant

単語

しょうじくんのストーリー

1

しょうじ: もしもし、まいちゃん？
ぼく、しょうじ。ねえ、
あした、ぼくのうちに
あそびに来ない？
あたらしいカセット
いっしょに聞かない？
まいこ: いいね。何時？
しょうじ: ええと... 二時はどう？
まいこ: オッケー。じゃあ、
あしたね! バイバイ。
しょうじ: バイバイ。

2

3

グーグー。

4

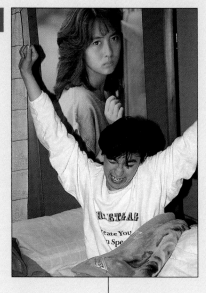

ああ〜あ。きもちいい。
うれしいな。
今日まいちゃんにあうんだ。

5

ええと... 今日のMTVは...

このへやちょっときたないな。
そうじして、それから...

6

しゅくだいして... ええと、
むずかしいな、これ。

7

リーン、リーン!

しょうじ: はい、もしもし、しょうじです。
くみこ: あ、くみこです。今日は。
ねえ、しょうじくん、これから
みんなでカラオケ行くの。
しょうじ: いいね。どこ行くの?
くみこ: ビッグエコー! しょうじくんも
来ない?
しょうじ: ううん、今はちょっと...
しゅくだいがたくさんあって...
ごめんね。

8

9

リーン、リーン!

もしもし、しょうじくん?
わたし、今日しょうじくんのうち、
行けないの。ごめんね。これから、
おばあちゃんのおみまい行くの。

11

そう... 来られない? ざんねんだなあ...
じゃあ..またね。

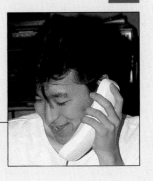

10

12

あ〜あ、つまらない。
そうじもしゅくだいもしたのに...
がっかりしちゃうよ...。

13

おにいちゃん、ここに来てもいい?
ともだちも?

14

えっ? ともだち?
中学生の...?
しかたがない...

おんなのこ: わあ! このおせんべい、おいしい!
ねえ、しょうじさん、うた、
うたってください。
しょうじ: えっ? ぼく一人で? オッケー…
おんなのこ: 中山美穂ちゃんのうた、うたって!
よく、美穂ちゃんのうた、うたう?
しょうじ: ううん、あんまりうたわない…
おんなのこ: でも、おねがい、おねがい!

わあ! じょうず! じょうず!
かっこいい! すてき!

しょうじ、きのうどうだった?
まいちゃんと…

まいちゃん、
来なかったけど…
おんなのこが三人来て…

17

へえ! おんなのこが三人?!

18

いいましょう 一

よくみほちゃんのうた、うたう？
ううん、あんまりうたわない。

一

二

三

四

五

Using the example as a guide, decide whether or not the activities illustrated are things that you do frequently.

> 例:
> A　よくおかし食べる?
> B　うん、よく食べる。
> 　　or
> 　　ううん、あんまり食べない。

一 さんぽ行く

二 ビデオ見る

三 トランプする

四 テニスする

五 CD聞く

六 ポップコーンつくる

Using the example as a guide, invite your friend to do the activities illustrated. They may accept or decline.

例:
A いっしょにさんぽ行かない?
B いいね。
　or
　ううん、今はちょっと.... ごめんね。

Using the example as a guide, explain
what you are going into town to buy.

例:
A 何しに行くの?
B ジャケット買いに行くの。

A 何しに行くの?
B ジャケット買いに行くんだ。

ううん、ぼく、
今ダイエット中...

おじいちゃん、
アイスクリーム
食べに行かない?

一 見に

二 食べに

三 (ともだちに)あいに

四 かえしに

五 聞きに

六 あそびに

After saying that you are going to town, explain why and
what you are going to do. Use the example as a guide.

例:
A 何しに行くの?
B えいが見に行くの。

A 何しに行くの?
B えいが見に行くんだ。

The following conversation takes place when you meet your friend on the street. After you have decided who will be A and who will be B, make up a conversation.

A	どこ行くの?					
B	本 ビデオ	かえしに	行くの。 行くんだ。			
A	どんな	本? ビデオ?				
B	ロマンス コメディー S.F.	の	本。 ビデオ。			
A	[B]さんは [B]くんは	いつも	ロマンス コメディー S.F.	の	本 ビデオ	読むね。 見るね。
	その	本 ビデオ	おもしろかった? よかった?			
B	うん、	おもしろかったよ。 よかったよ。	[A]さん、 [A]くん、	これから、何するの?		
A	べつに...					
B	じゃあ、いっしょに	ビデオショップ としょかん	行かない?			
A	ビデオショップ? としょかん?	オッケー。ねえ、	わたし、 ぼく、	あした 今日のごご こんばん		
	まちに ショッピングセンターに ともだちのうちに ビッグエコーに	えいが見に コンサート聞きに あそびに トランプしに うたいに	行くの。 行くんだ。			
	いっしょに行かない?					
B	あした? 今日のごご? こんばん?	ええと...	うん、 ううん、	いいよ。 あした 今日のごご こんばん	はちょっと...	

一 カラオケ行かない？

You are really keen to try some カラオケ at ビッグエコー, but your friend is very reluctant. They keep making all sorts of excuses about why it's not for them (e.g. it looks expensive, the songs are old, they don't want to sing by themselves, they're busy until 5.00, they're always hungry after school...). You will be able to find all that you need to convince them to come with you in the material about カラオケ. When you have overcome all of your friend's objections, arrange a time and place to meet them.

二 ビッグエコーでバイトするの。

You are about to start a バイト as the desk person at ビッグエコー. You are required to be able to answer lots of questions about the facilities. Your friend has offered to help you with your 'training' by asking you the sorts of questions that customers will ask. You will need to know things like:

· what times the studio is open
· what kind of rooms there are and how much they cost per hour
· how many 'singers' can use a room at one time
· whether customers can eat and drink while singing
· what kind of songs are on the 'menu'.

When you're able to give all of this information to your friend, you'll know that you're ready to start work.

What better way to beat the pressures and stress of work and school than to get together with some friends and... sing. Yes, sing!

That's what カラオケ is all about. Japanese people have always seen singing as a great way to socialise and to relax, and now カラオケ is the modern way to go about it. カラ means *empty*, and オケ is short for *orchestra*. The orchestra is not really empty, but it is missing something - a singer - and that's where you come in. You choose a song from the カラオケ menu, laser disc technology goes into full swing, and from the big speakers behind you come the sounds of the band. On the screen in front of you, under the trendy video clip, the words of the song appear. The words are progressively coloured in to show you where you should be singing - so concentrate, and don't get distracted by the video clip, which often does not have much to do with what you are singing about.

Don't be shy, you don't have to have a great voice. You'll see, all the other people there will encourage you with plenty of パチパチ in the instrumental breaks. You'll probably warm up, get a little carried away even, and start throwing in those gestures and mannerisms you usually save for when you're singing in the shower.

Originally, カラオケ was for men, looking to relax in dimly-lit city bars after a hard day at the office. You can still hear them there, singing their favourite ballads, even those quavery old Japanese folk songs - and loving it!

But these days カラオケ belongs to everyone. People even pop in for a quick sing during their lunch break. Romantic couples go for 'happy love' カラオケ, looking into each other's eyes and crooning affectionately. What better test of love could there be?

Why not get together a group of friends and hire out a カラオケ box for an hour? It's like a private room, with all the necessary equipment, as well as tables and chairs where the 'audience' can eat, drink and applaud in comfort.

There are walk-in boxes, drive-in boxes, home カラオケ sets... Now, there's an idea. Get your own set-up, and become a pop star in the privacy of your own home. Why not have a カラオケ party? You'll love it.

Remember, you don't have to be a show-off. You just have to enjoy good music and good company.

⊠ Here is a script for a radio commercial for Oodate's latest karaoke studio.

カラオケ行かない?

ビッグエコーは大館のカラオケ
スタジオだよ。あさ十一時からよる
十二時まで。いろんな人が来て
うたうの。しゅふやこどもはごご来て、
こうこうせいはほうかごよくうたいに
来るの。こうこうせいは七時までここで
あそんでもいい。七時から
かいしゃいんがたくさん来る。
デラックスルームは一時間4500円で、
エコノミールームは一時間3000円よ。
スタジオに六人はいれる。
スタジオの中でスナックを
食べてもいい。ジュースものめる。
うたのメニューがあって、
いろんなうたがうたえるの。
ダンスもできるよ。たのしいよ。

単語	
あさ	a.m.
よる	p.m.
いろんな	various
しゅふ	housewives
かいしゃいん	company employees
デラックスルーム	deluxe room
エコノミールーム	economy room
スタジオ	studio
スナック	snack
ジュース	juice, soft drink
うたのメニュー	list of available songs

いやだなあ、一人で…。

さおりちゃん、がんばって!

つぎはわたしたち…。

♫ とうほくのおばあちゃん…。♫

カラオケはたのしいな。
そのみちゃんはダンスがじょうずね。

イヨイヨ！
'カラオケスタジオ・ビッグエコー'
ご当地にOPEN！！
皆様のご来場をお待ちいたしております。

大学生[1]! 高校生[2]!
の皆さん[3]専用[4]

歌[5]しませんか？

買物[6]かえりに[7]

ご家族[8]専用

お父さん専用

歌[5]いたい!!

料金表		
エコノミールーム	使用時間	デラックスルーム
3000円	1時間	4500円
4500円	2時間	9000円
6000円	3時間	13500円

1	大学生	だいがくせい
2	高校生	こうこうせい
3	皆さん	みなさん
4	専用	せんよう private use
5	歌	うた
6	買物	かいもの
7	かえりに	on your way home
8	家族	かぞく

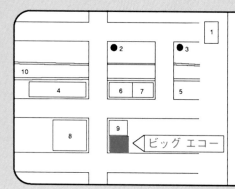

1　大館駅 (おおだてえき)
2　ガソリン スタンド
3　パチンコ サンワ
4　市立病院 (しりつ (City) びょういん)
5　公園 (こうえん)
6　レストラン ベルミート
7　小学校
8　スイミング スクール
9　ビービー ビデオ
10　長木川 (ながぎがわ)

今

Meaning: *now*

Readings
いま
こん

今・いま

今日・きょう
今月・こんげつ
今日は・こんにちは

 今 今

来

Meaning: *come*

Readings
く（る）
らい

来る・くる、来て・きて
来ない・こない、来られない・こられない

来月・らいげつ

 来 来

聞

Meaning: *hear, listen*

Readings
き（く）

聞く・きく
聞いて・きいて
聞かない・きかない

 聞 聞

読

Meaning: *read*

Readings
よ（む）

読む・よむ
読んで・よんで
読まない・よまない

 読 読

ー The plain verb form of 〜ません

You already know that when you say that you don't do something much, you use the 〜ません (negative) form of a verb.

e.g. あんまりべんきょうしません。
　　I don't study much.

The 〜ません form is *polite speech*. To make this statement in *plain speech*, you use the 〜ない form of the verb.

e.g. あんまりべんきょうしない。

To change *weak* verbs from 〜ません form into 〜ない form, you drop 〜ません and add ない.

e.g. 見ません　　　　見ない
　　できません　　　できない
　　いません　　　　いない

When you change *strong* verbs into 〜ない form, you drop 〜ません, change the final 'i' sound to 'a' and add ない. For example,

わかりません　わからない　らりるれろ
読みません　　読まない　　まみむめも
聞きません　　聞かない　　かきくけこ
まちません　　またない　　たちつてと

Look at the corresponding lines from the ひらがな table next to each example and you can see more clearly how these *strong* verbs change.

The 〜ない form for the group of *strong* verbs ending in 〜いません (such as 買いません) is made by dropping 〜ません and changing the final い to わ before adding ない.

e.g. 買いません　　　買わない
　　あらいません　　あらわない
　　うたいません　　うたわない

The *irregular* verbs are tricky and you should learn them carefully. Note for example that 来ません changes to 来ない.

〜ません form	〜ない form
weak verbs	
います	いない
(wear) きません	きない
食べません	食べない
でません	でない
見せません	見せない
strong verbs	
かえりません	かえらない
つくりません	つくらない
はしりません	はしらない
はいりません	はいらない
わかりません	わからない
あいません	あわない
あらいません	あらわない
うたいません	うたわない
買いません	買わない
たちません	たたない
まちません	またない
かきません	かかない
聞きません	聞かない
はきません	はかない
およぎません	およがない
あそびません	あそばない
のみません	のまない
読みません	読まない
かえしません	かえさない
かしません	かさない
はなしません	はなさない
irregular verbs	
ありません	ない
行きません	行かない
来ません	来ない
しません	しない

二　〜ない form as an invitation

Verbs in 〜ない form are also used when you invite a friend to do something.

e.g. いっしょにトランプしない？
　　　How about a game of cards?

A slight rising tone is used when you invite someone.

三　I can't do it!

Verbs such as 行ける, 来られる, うたえる and はなせる tell what you are *able to do*. Since these verbs in their *can* form end in '-eru', they become weak verbs. The ない form for these verbs is therefore made by dropping 〜ません and adding ない.

e.g. こんばんパーティーに行けない。
　　　I can't come to the party tonight.

　　　一人でうたえない。
　　　I can't sing by myself.

四　More about verbs

When you drop 〜ます (or 〜ません) from a verb, you are left with the stem of the verb. To say that you are going somewhere in order to do something, に行く (and に来る) are added to the verb stem.

e.g. まちへえいが見に行くの。
　　　I'm going to town to see a film.

　　　うちにあそびに来ない？
　　　How about coming over to my place?

　　　レストランへばんごはんを食べに行きます。
　　　We're going to the restaurant to have dinner.

In plain speech, you cannot drop に after the stem or に or へ after the place.

単語	
あそびに来る	to come and visit
うれしい	happy, pleased
おみまい	visiting someone who is sick or injured
おねがい!	please!
かえす	to return something
来なかった plain form of 来ませんでした	didn't come
しかたがない	that's too bad, it can't be helped
(そうじした)のに...	I've even (cleaned up)
だった plain form of でした	was
一人で (ひとりで)	by myself, alone
みんなで	altogether, with everyone

外来語(がいらいご)	
S.F. (エスエフ)	science fiction
カセット	cassette
コメディー	comedy
グーグー	...zzz!
ショッピングセンター	shopping centre
ポップコーン	popcorn
ラジカセ	radio-cassette player
ロマンス	romance

プチ・グルメで

くみちゃん、おそいなあ...

あっ、くみちゃん、ここ!

まいちゃん、おそくなってごめんね。まった?

ううん、そんなに...

三十分
まったよ。

ああ、のどかわいた。何かのもうよ。

うん、でもわたし、
おなかすいた。
プチグルメで何か食
べようよ。

うん、でも...

わたしダイエット中...

わあ！いろんなのみものがあるね。

わたし、グレープフルーツジュース。

そうねえ。じゃ、わたしもグレープフルーツジュース。

オス！まった？

二十五分まったよ。

ごめん、ごめん。

あっ、ねえ、くみちゃん、あそこにしょうじくんときみひろくんがいる。こっち来ない？よく見えるよ。

ああ、いいアイディアね。

見える？

うん、見える、見える。

何のもうかな...

あっ、まいちゃんがいる。

そう？ あっ、そばのテーブル
あいてるよ。あそこ行かない？

うん。

ごちゅうもんは？

ええと、クリームソーダを
一つとグレープフルーツ
ジュースを一つおねがい
します。

はい、クリームソーダとグレープ
フルーツジュースですね。

10

あれ？ このクリームソーダ、
ぼくのじゃないですよ。

あっ、どうもすみません。

11

いいよ。いいよ。
しかたがないよ。
ぼく、それものむ。

12

13

でもねえ...

14

ハーイ! まいちゃん、ジュースとソーダ、おいしかった。どうもごちそうさま!

15

えっ? ごちそうさま?

まいちゃん...しょうじくんたちののみものも...はらうの?

16

クリームソーダを二つとグレープフルーツジュースを三つですね。

しょうじくん、ひどい!

17

飲みものいろいろ

⑲オレンジジュース 300円
⑳グレープフルーツジュース 300円
⑯コカコーラ 200円
⑮アイスティー 280円
⑱レモンスカッシュ 300円
⑰ジンジャーエール 250円

Using the example as a guide, decide what you'll have to drink.

例:
A のどかわいたね。何かのもうよ。
B うん。何かのもう。

A 何のむの?
B わたし／ぼく、レモンスカッシュ。

フレッシュデザート

②フルーツパフェ 450円
⑤プチ小倉パフェ 380円
③チョコレートパフェ 450円
④プチヨーグルトパフェ 380円
①バニラアイスクリーム 300円

小倉・おぐら

Using the example as a guide, decide which dessert you'd like to have.

例:
A おなかすいたね。何か食べようよ。
B うん。何か食べよう。

A 何食べるの?
B わたし／ぼく、プチヨーグルトパフェ。

コーン・ラーメン　　580 円

えびフライセット　　1,280 円

やきそばとごはん　　680 円

おいしさ速達スピードメニュー

スピードビーフカレー　680 円

かつどん　　　　680円

㉑クリームソーダ 350円
㉒バナナヨーグルトシェーク
350円

キウイヨーグルトシェーク 350円

レモンティー
250 円

ホットコーヒー
250円

Look at the menu items pictured and use the example as a guide for placing your order.

例:
A　ごちゅうもんは?
B　スピードビーフカレーとホットコーヒー、おねがいします。
A　はい、スピードビーフカレーとホットコーヒーですね。

Talk about the prices on the menu, using the example as a guide.

例:

A　コーンラーメンはいくら?
B　580円よ。

A　コーンラーメンはいくら?
B　580円だよ。

ファンタスティック　フィーリ

ヤングのみんな! こんどのなつやすみ、何するの?
山のぼり? サーフィン?
ねえ、ディズニーランドに来ない?
たのしいイベントやアトラクションがまってるよ。

おもしろいショーを見に行かない?
カラフルなパレードはまい日三時から。
よるはエレクトリカルパレードや
スターライトファンタジー、それに
ディスコディズニーに行こうよ。

ダンスしない?

見える?

ううん、
見えない。

ううん、
しない。

おみやげもいろいろあるよ。
お父さんやお母さんにも
おみやげを買おうね。

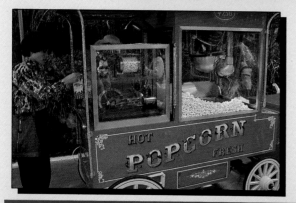

ディズニーランドのスナックはおいしいよ。
さあ! 食べよう! アメリカンテイスト!

エキサイティングでスリルいっぱいのアトラクション!
ロマンティックなファンタジーランドもすてきだよ。
しゃしんもたくさんとろうね。

そのみみ、かわいいね。

ウフフフ...

ともだちと、かぞくと、
ガールフレンドと、
ボーイフレンドと!さあ、
いっしょに来てね。
ファンタスティックフィーリング!

ハロー!

あのこ、
かわいいね。

単語			
ファンタスティック	fantastic	エレクトリカルパレード	Electrical Parade
フィーリング	feeling	スターライトファンタジー	Starlight Fantasy
ヤング	young	ディスコ	disco
サーフィン	surfing	テイスト	taste
イベント	event	エキサイティング	exciting
アトラクション	attraction	スリル	thrill
ショー	show	ファンタジーランド	Fantasy Land
カラフル	colourful, bright	ハロー	hello
パレード	parade		

いいましょう 三

	1		3		4		6		8		10	
7.00 ニュース		7.00 クイズ		7.00 まんが		7.00 ナイター		7.00 えいが		7.00 MTV ジャパン		7

Using the example as a guide, suggest a TV program to watch.

例:
A　何見ようか。
B　ニュース見ようよ。

一

レイダース

二

バック・トゥ・ザ・フューチャー

三

ブラック・レイン

四

ゴッド・ファーザー

Which video would you like to borrow?
Suggest a title, using the example as a guide.

例:
A　何かりようか。
B　レイダースかりようよ。

一

マインド・
ユニバース

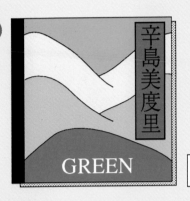

二

GREEN

グリーン

三

光Genji

サンキュー

四

森川美穂

ポップ・ザ・トップ

五

ドゥランジャー

Which CD would you like to listen to?
Using the example as a guide, suggest a title from the covers illustrated.

例:
A マインド・ユニバース聞こうよ。
B うん、聞こう。

Using the example as a guide, work out which CD you'll buy for しょうじくん.

例:
A しょうじくんにマインド・ユニバースのＣＤ買おうよ。
B うん、いいね。そうしよう。

いいましょう 四

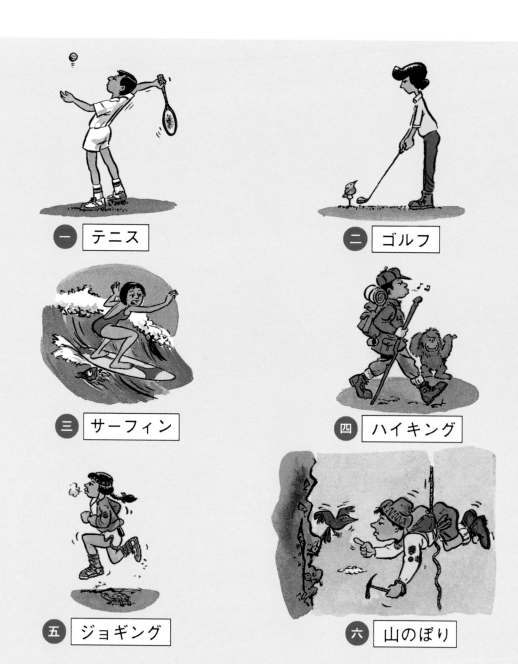

一 テニス	二 ゴルフ
三 サーフィン	四 ハイキング
五 ジョギング	六 山のぼり

Suggest an activity to do with your friend next Sunday.
Use the example as a guide.

例:

A こんどの日よう日、いっしょにテニスしようよ。
B うん、そうしよう。
　　or
　　ごめんね。わたし、山のぼりするの。

A こんどの日よう日、いっしょにテニスしようよ。
B うん、そうしよう。
　　or
　　ごめん。ぼく、山のぼりするんだ。

At the restaurant you are talking with your friend about the weekend.
Decide who will be A and who will be B and make up a conversation.

A	おなかすいたね。 のどかわいたね。	何か	食べようよ。 のもうよ。
B	うん、何か	食べよう。 のもう。	
A	何	食べるの? のむの?	
B	わたし ぼく	ミックスピザ。 マロンパフェ。 オレンジジュース。 レモンスカッシュ。	
A	じゃ、わたし ぼく	フルーツパフェ。 ツナサラダ。 ジンジャーエール。 クリームソーダ。	

B	すみません。	ミックスピザ マロンパフェ フルーツパフェ ツナサラダ オレンジジュース レモンスカッシュ ジンジャーエール クリームソーダ	と　ミックスピザ マロンパフェ フルーツパフェ ツナサラダ オレンジジュース レモンスカッシュ ジンジャーエール クリームソーダ	おねがいします。

A	ねえ、	こんどの土よう日、 こんどの日よう日、	いっしょに　ハイキング サイクリング ＣＤ えいが	しようよ。 聞こうよ。 見ようよ。

B	ごめんね。	15日 24日 10日 8日	は　母 父 あね あに	のたんじょう日で、パーティー	するの。 するんだ。
	レストランにごはん食べに	行くの。 行くんだ。			
A	ああ、そう。いいね。				

⊗⊗

何月何日？

たんじょう日は四月四日よ。

たんじょう日は七月七日だよ。

わたしのたんじょう日は五月十三日よ。

ぼくのたんじょう日は
一月十日だよ。

 例:
A おたんじょう日は何月何日?
B 十一月一日よ。

 A たんじょう日は何月何日?
B 十一月一日だよ。

Now that you know how to ask the date of someone's birthday, why not find out about your classmates' birthdays. Use the examples as a guide.

Days of the month

何日　なんにち

一日	ついたち	十七日	じゅうしちにち
二日	ふつか	十八日	じゅうはちにち
三日	みっか	十九日	じゅうくにち
四日	よっか	二十日	はつか
五日	いつか	二十一日	にじゅういちにち
六日	むいか	二十二日	にじゅうににち
七日	なのか	二十三日	にじゅうさんにち
八日	ようか	二十四日	にじゅうよっか
九日	ここのか	二十五日	にじゅうごにち
十日	とおか	二十六日	にじゅうろくにち
十一日	じゅういちにち	二十七日	にじゅうしちにち
十二日	じゅうににち	二十八日	にじゅうはちにち
十三日	じゅうさんにち	二十九日	にじゅうくにち
十四日	じゅうよっか	三十日	さんじゅうにち
十五日	じゅうごにち	三十一日	さんじゅういちにち
十六日	じゅうろくにち		

おたんじょう日
おめでとう!

ありがとう。でも、
ぼくのたんじょう日は
ようかだよ。

ゴールデンウィークについて

四月二十九日から五月五日までの一週間はゴールデンウィークです。四月二十九日はみどりの日、五月三日はけんぽうきねん日、そして、五月五日は子どもの日です。五月のおてんきはとてもいいです。

かぞくはみんなででかけます。よくりょこうもします。だから、日本では、みんなゴールデンウィークをたのしみにしています。

単語

ゴールデンウィーク	Golden Week
りょこうする	to travel, to take a trip
たのしみにしている	to look forward to

		Japanese National Holidays・国民の祝日		

1月1日	元旦 (がんたん)	New Year's Day
1月15日	成人の日 (せいじんのひ)	Coming-of-Age Day
2月11日	建国記念の日 (けんこくきねんのひ)	National Foundation Day
3月21日 *ごろ	春分の日 (しゅんぶんのひ)	Spring Equinox
4月29日	緑の日 (みどりのひ)	Greenery Day
5月3日	憲法記念日 (けんぽうきねんび)	Constitution Day
5月5日	子供の日 (こどものひ)	Children's Day
9月15日	敬老の日 (けいろうのひ)	Respect-for-the-Aged Day
9月23日 *ごろ	秋分の日 (しゅうぶんのひ)	Autumn Equinox
10月10日	体育の日 (たいいくのひ)	Health-Sports Day
11月3日	文化の日 (ぶんかのひ)	Culture Day
11月23日	勤労感謝の日 (きんろうかんしゃのひ)	Labour Thanksgiving Day
12月23日	天皇誕生日 (てんのうたんじょうび)	Emperor's Birthday

*〜ごろ   about, around

Most Japanese people know the dates of their national holidays. You can practise asking and telling dates by talking about the Japanese national holidays. Use the examples below as a guide.

A　子どもの日は何月何日？
B　5月5日よ。

A　子どもの日は何月何日？
B　5月5日だよ。

子どもの日

子どもの日 is celebrated on May 5. It is sometimes known as たんごのせっく and was originally just a boys' festival. Now it is a national holiday held in honour of all children.

こいのぼり are flown from houses where there are boy children. The carp streamers remind boys to imitate these strong, determined fish that swim upstream, against the current. Most families with daughters don't bother with こいのぼり, probably because girls already have strength and determination and don't need to be reminded!!

If the こいのぼり are not enough to remind children that life can be a battle, then the 五月にんぎょう should do the trick! These dolls in samurai warrior armour are usually placed on a sort of stand and surrounded with weapons from the samurai era. 五月にんぎょう make an impressive 子どもの日 display but not everyone has them because they are very expensive.

Part of the celebration is eating special 子どもの日 cakes. (It's the only way to eat carp!)

Visiting colonels sometimes dress in samurai armour for 子どもの日.

上

Meaning: *up, above, on*

Readings
うえ

テーブルの上・テーブルのうえ

下

Meaning: *down, under*

Readings
した、くだ(さい)

ベッドの下・ベッドのした
下さい・ください

子

Meaning: *child*

Readings
こ

子供・こども
子供の日・こどものひ

一 ～ましょう in plain form

To suggest doing something with your friends, you can use the plain speech form of ～ましょう.

e.g. ビデオかりようか。
Shall we rent a video?
ううん、CD 聞こうよ。
No, let's listen to a CD.

By now you will know that the way the plain form is made depends on what kind of verb you are dealing with. For *weak* verbs, the plain form of ～ましょう is made by dropping ましょう and adding よう.

e.g. 食べましょう　　食べよう
　　 かりましょう　　かりよう
　　 でかけましょう　でかけよう

When changing *strong* verbs into the plain form of ～ましょう, you drop ましょう and change the final 'i' sound into an 'oo' sound. For example;

かえりましょう　かえろう　らりるれろ
買いましょう　　買おう　　あいうえお
聞きましょう　　聞こう　　かきくけこ
あそびましょう　あそぼう　ばびぶべぼ
読みましょう　　読もう　　まみむめも

Look at the corresponding lines from the ひらがな table next to each example and you can see more clearly how these strong verbs change. Look at these further examples.

はなしましょう　はなそう　さしすせそ
まちましょう　　まとう　　たちつてと

You will also need to know how to make this form from the plain present or dictionary form. The verb table shows these changes.

いっしょに
山のぼり
しようよ。

うん、そうしよう。

plain present	～ましょう form	plain よう/おう form
weak verbs		
かりる	かりましょう	かりよう
しめる	しめましょう	しめよう
食べる	食べましょう	食べよう
ねる	ねましょう	ねよう
見せる	見せましょう	見せよう
strong verbs		
とる	とりましょう	とろう
はいる	はいりましょう	はいろう
はしる	はしりましょう	はしろう
わたる	わたりましょう	わたろう
あう	あいましょう	あおう
うたう	うたいましょう	うたおう
たつ	たちましょう	たとう
まつ	まちましょう	まとう
かく	かきましょう	かこう
聞く	聞きましょう	聞こう
あそぶ	あそびましょう	あそぼう
のむ	のみましょう	のもう
読む	読みましょう	読もう
かえす	かえしましょう	かえそう
はなす	はなしましょう	はなそう
irregular verbs		
行く	行きましょう	行こう
来る	来ましょう	来よう
する	しましょう	しよう

Note that 来ましょう becomes 来よう.

二 More about に

When you buy something for someone, the particle に means *for* and it follows the name or title of the person you are buying for.

e.g. しょうじくんにカラオケテープ
買おう。
Let's get a karaoke tape for Shooji.

Expressions	
いいアイディアね	that's a good idea!
おなかすいた	I'm hungry
ごちゅうもんは?	your order?
そうしよう	let's do that
どうもごちそうさま	thank you very much
のどかわいた	I'm thirsty
ぼくのじゃないです	it's not mine
まった?	have you been waiting long?

単語	
あいてる	to be vacant
いっぱい	full
かりる	to borrow, to rent
こっち	here
こんど	next
そんなに	not that much
何か (なにか)	something
のみもの	drink
はらう	to pay
見える	to be able to see

何見ようか。

ミッキーレビュー
見に行こうよ。
おもしろそう!

富士山見える?

ファンタスティックだね。

宮島へ

⊗⊗

ぼく、しんじ。広島にすんでる。
広島高校の三年生だよ。みんな
ゴールデンウィークに何したの?
ぼくは五日にガールフレンドの
なおみちゃんと宮島にあそびに
行ったんだ。宮島は、きれいな
しまで、広島から一時間はんぐらい
かかる。しゃしんをたくさん
とったよ。これから見せるね。

1

2

広島えきからフェリーのりば
まででんしゃで行った。

なおみ: あっ、フェリーが来た。

3

4

このしゃしんの右がわに
ゆうめいな宮島のとりいが
見える。

宮島には、しかがたくさんいる。

しんじ: あっ! ぼくたちもしかに
せんべいあげようよ。

しずかにして! はい! チーズ!!

とりいのそばに小学生がいた。
とってもうるさかった。せんせいは
たいへんだね。

ぼくたちもとりいのしゃしんを
たくさんとった。

なおみ: 見て! あのこいのぼり
大きいね。

それから、山の上の大聖院を見た。
このおてらはとてもふるい。

なおみちゃんはえまにねがい
ごとをかいた。

しんじ: なおみちゃん、どんなねがい
　　　ごとかいたの？
なおみ: ないしょ...
しんじ: ぼくとけっこんしたい？
なおみ: ばかねえ。

10

ロープウェーの中には、なおみちゃんと
ぼくだけ....むねがドキドキした。

なおみ: わああ! 高い、高い!
　　　きれいね。
しんじ: ぼく...　むねがドキドキ
　　　するよ。
なおみ: どうして？こわい？

しんじ: ううん、なおみちゃん、
　　　かわいい...

11

12

この日のてんきはよかった。だから、
けしきはとてもすばらしかった。
小さいしまがたくさん見えた。

13

三時のフェリーでかえった。とてもたのしい日
だった。またなおみちゃんとデートしたいなあ。

単語			
えま	wooden tablet to write wishes on	しま	island
おてら	Buddhist temple	とりい	Shinto gateway
しか	deer	ねがいごと	prayer or wish

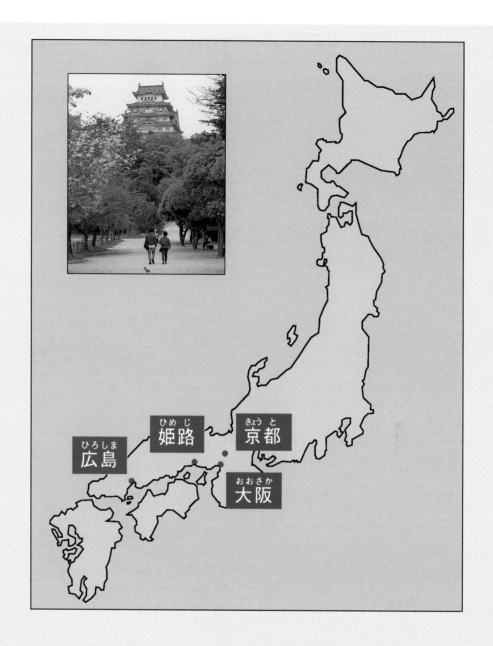

Where did you go during Golden Week?
Using the example as a guide, talk about where you went.

例:

A ゴールデンウィークに何したの?
B りょこうしたの。
A どこ行ったの?
B 広島行ったの。

A ゴールデンウィークに何したの?
B りょこうしたんだ。
A どこ行ったの?
B 広島行ったんだ。

おてら

二

 ドイツのバンド 三

姫路 四

(お)しろ 五

 六

広島 七　へいわこうえん

八

おこのみやき 九

Talk about what you did at these places, using the example as a guide.
The verbs given in the box below may be of assistance.

食べた	行った	見た	とった	買った
(と)はなした	聞いた	見に行った	食べに行った	

例:
 A　京都で何したの?
B　おてら見たの。

 A　京都で何したの?
B　おてら見たんだ。

たいいくさい　　　　　　　　　　5月10日　あめ

　今日は学校のたいいくさいだった。あめだった。だから、たいいくかんの中でしたんだ。かくチーム、バナーをつくった。三週間かかったんだ。ぼくたちはGチームだった。Eチームのバナーはすごかった。みんなよくがんばった。

わあ! すごいえい語!
あのえい語わかる?
ううん、ぜんぜんわかんない。

一年生はみんなちゃんとスポーツユニフォームをきていた。まじめだね。

でも、三年生はみんなへんなかっこうだった。

おもしろいイベントがたくさんあった。ぼくは二人三きゃくが大すきだ。

8 ひるやすみにきょうしつでおべんとうを食べた。

9 それから、ぼくたちはきょうしつでトランプした。

ウノはおもしろいなあ!

10

あっ、お金わすれた! ざんねん!

11

ともだちのちあきくんはじどうはんばいきでジュースを買った。

12

ごごのイベントは二時からはじまった。ダンスコンテストはとてもおもしろかった。Gチームのダンスはすばらしかった。もちろん一ばんだった。

13

14

そのつぎはつなひきだった。Gチームのおんなの子はまけたけど、おとこはかった。

15

三時はんにひょうしょうしきがあった。ぼくたちのチームがゆうしょうした。とてもうれしかった。

単語	
二人三きゃく(ににんさんきゃく)	three-legged race
つなひき	tug of war
ひょうしょうしき	prize ceremony
ゆうしょうする	to win the championship

きのうこうえん行ったんだよ。

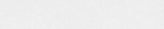

一　　　　　二　　　　　三

What do you do when it's raining outside?
Using the example as a guide, ask and say what you did yesterday.

例:

A　きのうはあめだったね。何したの?
B　きょうしつでトランプしたの。

A　きのうはあめだったね。何したの?
B　きょうしつでトランプしたんだ。

A　きのうはあめでしたね。何をしましたか。
B　きょうしつでトランプをしました。

Using the example as a guide, talk about what
you did yesterday when the weather was fine.

例:

A きのうはいいおてんきだったね。何したの?
B こうていでブラスバンドのれんしゅうしたの。

A きのうはいいてんきだったね。何したの?
B こうていでブラスバンドのれんしゅうしたんだ。

A きのうはいいおてんきでしたね。何をしましたか。
B こうていでブラスバンドのれんしゅうをしました。

時間割り (わ)

	月	火	水	木	金	土
1 2 3 4	すう学 こく語 けいざい か学	えい語 ぶつり こく語 たいいく	ちり びじゅつ えい語 れきし	か学 けいざい すう学 れきし	こく語 ぶつり えい語 すう学	ぶつり おんがく こく語 ちり
ひるやすみ						
5 6	えい語 ちり	すう学 か学	すう学 クラブ	たいいく こく語	れきし けいざい	

Using the example as a guide, talk about
しょうじくんの時間割り(わ).

例:
A 月よう日の一時間目(め)は何だった?
B すう学だった。

A 月よう日の一時間目(め)は何でしたか。
B すう学でした。

This dialogue takes place at the lockers before school.
Decide who will be A and who will be B and make up a conversation.

A	きのうは	あめ いいてんき	だったね。何したの?					
B	うちで へやで	べんきょうした しゅくだいした 本読んだ	の。 んだ。	おもしろかったよ。 たのしかったよ。 つまらなかったよ。 よかったよ。	[A]くんは? [A]さんは?			
	川に 山に	サイクリングに行った ハイキングに行った あそびに行った						
A	ぼくは わたしは	あね あに おとうと いもうと	の	高校 中学	の	やきゅう じゅうどう サッカー	のしあい	見に行ったの。 見に行ったんだ。
B	へえ?!　いいね。	おねえさん おにいさん おとうとさん いもうとさん	の	高校 中学	かった?			
A	うん、かったよ。 ううん、まけたよ。							
B	よかったね。 ざんねんだったね。	今日の一時間目は何?						
A	すう学 えい語 けいざい ぶつり	のテスト!						
B	テスト?!	かわいそう! いやだね!	きのう、べんきょうした?					
A	ううん、ぜんぜん。	すう学 えい語 けいざい ぶつり	はやさしいよ!					

ひるやすみ

B	[A]さん、 [A]くん、	すう学 えい語 けいざい ぶつり	のテスト、どうだった?		
A	だめだった。 むずかしかった。	ああ、おなかすいた。おべんとう		食べに行こうよ。 買いに行こうよ。	

じんじゃとてら

Hi! My name is たみこ. I don't really think of myself as a religious person, but here I am at a じんじゃ, a しんとう shrine, reading my おみくじ along with the thousands of other people who have come here. I am not sure I really believe in these fortunes, but I always buy one when I go to a shrine that has them. This shrine has a really good reputation for bringing good luck, so I hope it works.

Before you get your おみくじ you roll this barrel sort of thing until a stick with a number pops out. This gives you the number of the おみくじ you have to buy.

After you have read your おみくじ you tie it onto the むすび木, the sacred tree. Don't ask me why. It's just what you do.

People often just pop into a じんじゃ when they're passing by. There are thousands of them around Japan. They are just everywhere. In the じんじゃ you pull the rope to ring the bell and clap your hands to let the かみさま know you are there. The かみさま are the gods. They are everywhere, in everything. I usually ask them to keep me safe, especially when I am driving. I have a charm from a じんじゃ in my car.

You know you are at a じんじゃ because they always have とりい gates. You know what they are, don't you? You must have seen them. When you pass through these gates you know you are in a holy place.

As I said, じんじゃ are everywhere. This one is in a shopping centre. People like to pop in, just to acknowledge the presence of the かみさま, just to keep in touch.

In しんとう it is important to be clean before you meet the かみさま. You can pour this water over your hands, but most people seem to have a drink. しんとう means *the way of the gods*. I just think it is part of everyday life.

But when people ask me what religion I am, I usually say Buddhist. Well, I'm both, しんとう and Buddhist. Most Japanese people are. I know visitors to Japan are often surprised to see Buddhist おてら and Shinto じんじゃ in the same grounds, but that is the way religion is in Japan.

Take my mother, for example. She would never think of starting a new year without a visit to our じんじゃ to get the blessing of the かみさま. And here she is at the Buddhist altar at home with photos of her father. She has a しんとう altar as well. She made sure that I understood about the かみさま and the じんじゃ and the おてら and everything. I think most Japanese parents do.

I often visit Buddhist おてら. They are always more elaborate than じんじゃ and there are always crowds of people there. You can buy おみくじ, and also えま. They are like wooden plaques and you write your wishes on them. When I was a student I always asked for help at exam time. At the last おてら I went to, I asked for a good husband. I'm still waiting!

At the おてら you always wave the incense over yourself. This is to keep evil away from you. It has worked pretty well for me so far, I think.

The pagoda is an important Buddhist symbol. The five levels represent the five elements - sky, wind, fire, water and earth.

So, like most Japanese people, I'm a bit of a mixture when it comes to religion. I will have a しんとう wedding ceremony and, when the time comes, a Buddhist funeral.

年

Meaning: *year*

Readings
とし
ねん

今年・ことし

来年・らいねん
一年生・いちねんせい

年 年

生

Meaning: *student*

Readings

せい

大学生・だいがくせい
高校生・こうこうせい
中学生・ちゅうがくせい

生 生

高

Meaning: *high, tall, expensive*

Readings
たか(い)
こう

高い山・たかいやま
高い本・たかいほん

高校・こうこう

高 高

一　きのうどこ行った?

Test your skill as an investigative reporter. You have exactly one minute to get as much information as possible out of a classmate about what they did yesterday. It is up to you to keep the questions coming and not be put off, even if your interviewee is not being all that helpful. You can ask about places, times, people and activities (e.g. sport, entertainment, food, shopping). The judging panel will be looking for the interviewer who thinks of the most questions and extracts the most information.

二　どこ?

In *Kimono 3*, you have 'visited' lots of places (e.g. cities such as 大館 and 弘前, various shops, places such as ディズニーランド, ビッグエコー). Make up five statements about a visit to one of these places, with each statement giving a further clue about where you have been. See how many clues it takes for your classmates to guess where it was. In the example below, the mystery destination was ミスタードーナツ. The questions in brackets were guesses people made as the clues were given.

1 コーヒーのんだ。(ともだちのうちだった? コーヒーショップだった?)
2 ともだちとはなした。(学校だった?)
3 メニュー読んだ。(レストランだった?)
4 くみこさんのおねえさんにあった。(大学だった?)
5 ドーナツ食べた。

三　金よう日の三時間目は何だった?

Challenge your friend to a test on your timetable for last week. You say a certain day and period and your friend has to tell you what subject they did. Take it in turns asking and answering and see how long you can go without making a mistake.

じゃんけん is a really popular game in Japan, but not only with children - adults like playing it too. The right hand forms the paper, scissors or rock while the left is kept free to score. じゃんけん is used to help settle major issues in life, like who is 'it', who goes first and who gets the front seat in the car.

パー

グー

チョキ

日本の子どもたちは、じゃんけんがすきです。じゃんけんはおもしろいあそびです。「じゃんけんポン!」か「じゃんけんポイ!」といって、グーかチョキかパーをだします。グーはいしのかたちをつくります。チョキは、はさみのかたち、そして、パーは、かみのかたちをつくります。グーはチョキにかちますが、パーにまけます。チョキはパーにかちますが、グーにまけます。パーはグーにかちますが、チョキにまけます。

単語	
いって	from いう, to say
だす	to put out
いし	rock
かたち	shape

ー Plain speech ー past tense

Look at the following changes made to the verb *listen* when it is used in plain speech:

聞きます　　　聞く
聞きません　　聞かない
聞きましょう　聞こう
聞いています　聞いてる

To tell a friend that you have heard or listened to something, you will need to change 聞きました to plain speech. This is not as difficult as the changes you have learnt previously ー you simply put the verb into -て form and change the て ending to た.

e.g. 聞きました　聞いて　聞いた

This way of forming the past tense plain form of verbs is the same for weak, strong and irregular verbs.

e.g. 見ました　　　見て　　　見た
買いました　　買って　　買った
来ました　　　来て　　　来た

You already know the past tense of い adjectives.

e.g. けしきはすばらしかったです。
The scenery was fantastic.

To put this into plain form you drop です.

e.g. けしきはすばらしかった。

For な adjectives and nouns, you form the past tense by changing です to でした.

e.g. あれはへんでした。
That was strange.

きのうはあめでした。
It rained yesterday.

To put these sentences into plain form, you change でした to だった.

e.g. あれはへんだった。
きのうはあめだった。

単語

一ばん	first, number one
かく〜	each, every
かっこう	appearance, look
けしき	scenery
これから	and now, from now
こわい	scared, scary
(お)せんべい	cracker biscuits
そのつぎ	after that
じどうはんばいき	vending machine
ちゃんと	perfectly, properly
だけ〜	only, just
ないしょ	secret
ばか	don't talk rubbish!
ぼくたち	we (male speaking)
まじめ(な)	conscientious, serious
わかんない	= わからない

外来語 (がいらいご)

コンテスト	contest
チーム	team
フェリー	ferry
バナー	banner
バンド	band
ブラスバンド	brass band
ユニフォーム	uniform
ロープウェー	rope way

学校の単語

けいざい	economics
こく語	Japanese language
たいいくさい	annual sportsday
しあい	match, game
〜時間め	counter for periods or classes
時間わり	timetable
ぶつり	physics

Verbs

あげる	to give to someone
がんばる	to try hard
わすれる	to forget
まける	to lose, to be defeated
かつ	to win
むねがドキドキする	to have one's heart beat madly

どっちがいい？

ピンクのとオレンジの、どっちがいい？

どっちもいいね。

1

A ピンクのとオレンジのと、
　どちらがいいですか。
B どちらもいいですね。

きいろいのとあおいの、どっちがいい？

きいろいほうがいいね。

2

3

A きいろいのとあおいのと、
　どちらがいいですか。
B きいろいほうがいいですね。

みどりのとしろいの、どっちがいい？

みどりのほうがいいね。

4

A みどりのとしろいのと、どちらがいいですか。
B みどりのほうがいいですね。

どっちがいい?

一

二

三

四

五

六

七

Which coloured item do you prefer? Using the example as a guide,
give your choice. The colours given in the box may be helpful.

カーキー khaki	ベージュ beige	むらさき purple

例:
A オレンジのとチェックの、どっちがいい?
B オレンジのほうがいいね。

いいましょう 二

一 | かつどん

てんどん

二 | Hぐみのバナー

Fぐみのバナー

三 | すし

やきざかな

五 | ローラースケート

ダンス

四

Using the examples as a guide, ask someone which of these two things they prefer.

They may like both.	They may choose one.
例：	例：
A かつどんとてんどん、どっちがすき？ B どっちもすき。	A かつどんとてんどん、どっちがすき？ B かつどんのほうがすき。 or てんどんよりかつどんのほうがすき。

ドッグコンテスト

1

オス! ぼくチャーリー。

2

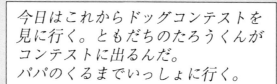

これはぼくのパパだよ。ぼくは
かぞくの中でパパが一ばんすき。

3

今日はこれからドッグコンテストを
見に行く。ともだちのたろうくんが
コンテストに出るんだ。
パパのくるまでいっしょに行く。

4

パパ、はやく、はやく! おくれるよ。

このすごいくるまを見て!
だれのくるまかな?

さいしょはしろいいぬのコンテストだ。

あのいぬ、いいね。

そうかな？あのいぬ
よりハンドラーの
ほうがかわいいよ。

たろうくんのコンテストは二ばんめだ。

つまらないなあ。

そのいぬとそのいぬ、
どっちがいい？

あっ！たろうがいるよ。
いつもゆうしょうするんだ。

でも、ぼくたちも今日はかっこいいよ。

第
九
課

百二十九

えゝと... どれが一ばんいいかな?

右のいぬはどう?

そうだねえ。

9

10

ぼく、たろう。今年も一ばんの
トロフィーをもらったよ。ぼくは
せかいで一ばんかっこいいいぬだよ。

ねえ、たろうくん、ぼく、これから
ヘアカットしに行くよ。

こんばんのパーティー行くの?

えっ?つかれた? えっ?
ダイエット中? うそ!

11

12

あれ? たろうはどこ?

ぼく、ほんとうは
にくよりやきとりの
ほうがいいなあ...

単語	
(コンテスト)に出る	to enter (a contest)
ハンドラー	handler
ゆうしょうする	to win the championship
トロフィー	trophy

 いぬ

 ビル

 こい

 とりい

 とりい

You are really excited to see these things.
Talk about them, using the example as a guide.
The adjectives given in the box may be helpful.

いい	大きい	小さい	高い
あたらしい	すばらしい	ハイテクな	

例:
A わあ、見て、見て！ あのいぬ!
B うん、日本で一ばんいいいぬよ。

A わあ、見て、見て！ あのいぬ!
B うん、日本で一ばんいいいぬだよ。

一 くつ

三 パーマコース

HAIR STUDIO
J & K

MENU
パーマコース
ナチュラルコース・5500
オリジナルコース・6000
スペシャルコース・6500
クイーンコース・7000
（カット＋パーマ＋ブロー）
カットコース
オリジナルカット・2800
（カット＋ブロー）

二 ブラウス

四 シャツ

五 こおり

Which item do you like best? Using the examples as a guide, make your decision.

You may like them all.	You may not like any of them.
例:	例:
A どれが一ばんいい? B そうね。ぜんぶいい。	A どれが一ばんいい? B そうね。ぜんぶよくないよ。
A どれが一ばんいい? B そうだね。ぜんぶいい。	A どれが一ばんいい? B そうだね。ぜんぶよくないよ。

You may pick the one you like the best.

例:

A どれが一ばんいい?
B そうね。このくつが一ばんいいね。

 A どれが一ばんいい?
B そうだね。このくつが一ばんいいね。

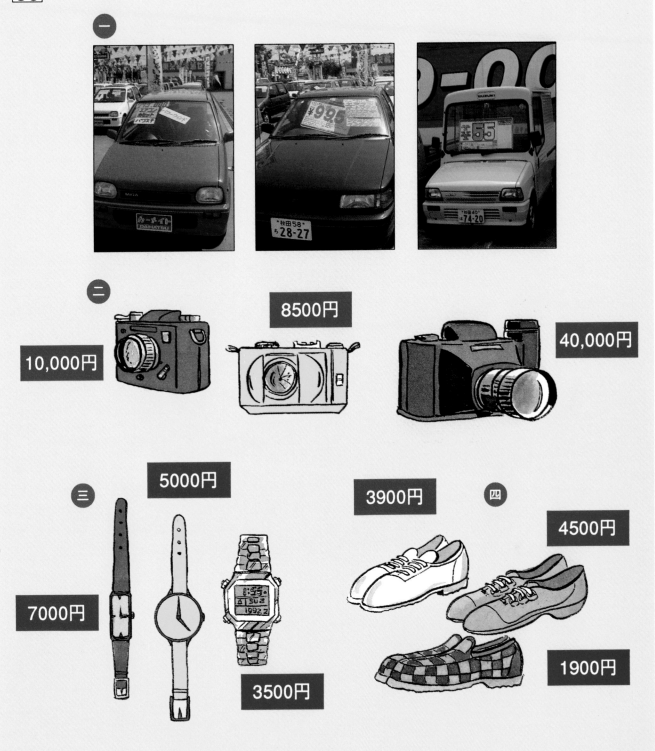

一

二

8500円

10,000円

40,000円

三

5000円

四

3900円

4500円

7000円

3500円

1900円

Which is the most expensive item from each group?
Using the example as a guide, make your decision.

例:
A　あかいのときいろいのとあおいの、どれが一ばん高い?
B　あおいくるまが一ばん高い。

ぼく、まこと。まいこのあにだ。いま大阪にすんでる。
ゴールデンウィークにともだち四人と京都にあそびに行った...

1

...ぼくはきょ年、オーストラリアに
行って、一年間えい語をべんきょうした。
このラグビーシャツはオーストラリアで
買ったんだ。ともだちのすすむは
ロサンジェルスでラグビーシャツを
買った。でも、ぼくのシャツのほうが
かっこいい。
　このしゃしんの左がわのがいこく人は
リチャード。オーストラリア人だ。
おんなの子たちは、みなこさんと
えりこさんで、ぼくとおなじかいしゃに
つとめてる。

2

大阪から京都までくるまで
行った。ちゅうしゃじょうは
とてもこんでた。
一時間ぐらいまった。

3　どこも人がたくさんいた。

4

ゆうめいなおてらのまえで
しゃしんをとった。

5

京都にはおてらやじんじゃやきれいな
にわがたくさんある。リチャードは
びっくりした。

6

のどがかわいた。だから洛匠に
入った。洛匠は京都ではゆうめいな
きっさてんだ。

ぼくはこいのチャンピオン!

7

にわにこいのいけがある。ぼく、
ここのにわが大すきだ。ここに
日本で一ばんすばらしいこいが
いる。

ぼくのトロフィーを見て。
たくさんもらったよ。

8

それから、祇園に行った。きれいなまいこさんを見たが...

しゃしんをとらないで！

それでもリチャードはしゃしんをとった。

一時にみんなはおなかがすいた。
ひるごはんはうどんを食べに行った。
このみせのうどんはおいしい。だから、
いつもそとで人がたくさんまってる。

あ〜あ、おなかすいた。
はやく食べたい。

このとりいはせかいで一ばん大きい。
リチャードはびっくりして、おなじ
しゃしんを十五まいとった。

すごいなあ、このとりい！

13

平安神宮はとてもカラフルだけど、
にわはしずかですばらしい。

14

15

へんなヤツにあった。

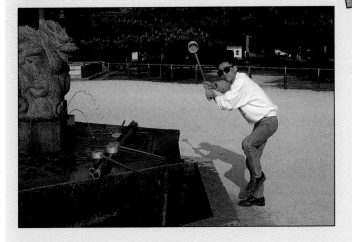

リチャードはおみくじを買って、
木にむすんだ。
よる十一時はんに大阪についた。

16

単語	
おてら	Buddhist temple
じんじゃ	Shinto shrine
まいこさん	apprentice geisha
とりい	gateway to Shinto shrine
おみくじ	written fortune
木にむすぶ	to tie on a tree

This is the dialogue from a television quiz show. Decide who will be A (the quiz master) and who will be B (the contestant) and make up a conversation.

A	みなさん、こんばんは！　おげんきですか。			
	今日のコンテスタントは	ジェニー・クレイグさん ロン・ピーターソンさん クリス・エバンズさん	です。	
	では、	ジェニーさん、 ロンさん、 クリスさん、	いいですか。	
B	はい。			
A	じゃ、しつもん一。しんかんせんとバスとくるまと、どれが一ばんはやいですか。			
B	しんかんせん バス くるま	が一ばん　はやいです。		
A	ピンポン！ ブー！	じゃ、しつもん二。ゴールデンウィークはいつからですか。		
B	4月29日 5月5日	からです。		

A	ピンポン！ ブー！	つぎのしつもん。	京都と奈良と 九州と北海道と CDとレコードと	どっちが	ふるい あたらしい 大きい
	ですか。				
B	京都 奈良 北海道 九州 CD レコード	より	奈良 京都 九州 北海道 レコード CD	のほうが	ふるい あたらしい 大きい	です。

A				
ピンポン！ ブー！	はい！ あなたのスコアは	0てん 5てん 10てん 15てん	です。	

ざんねんでした。
おめでとうございます！

プライズは	けしゴム スポーツカー コピーペン	か	はさみ ヨット ラジカセ	ですよ。

どちらがいいですか。

B		
ええと、	けしゴム、 はさみ、 スポーツカー、 ヨット、 コピーペン、 ラジカセ、	おねがいします。

単語	
コンテスタント	contestant
しつもん	question
てん	points
スコア	score
プライズ	prize

ブー or ピンポン？

In a quiz show, when you get a question wrong, you get the buzzer, ブー. If you get it right, you get the bell, ピンポン. But ブー and ピンポン have also found their way into the everyday language of lots of young Japanese people. Say something they disagree with and you're likely to get a ブー. Say the right thing and you'll be rewarded with ピンポン.

一

Why not run a quiz program in your class? You can all contribute questions (written in 日本語 of course) and find out who is the チャンピオン. Here are a couple of quiz questions to get you started.

e.g. せかいでどれが一ばん高い山ですか。
日本でどれが一ばん大きいまちですか。

二

In your classroom, set up a number of club information desks. Students in charge of a desk have to be ready to explain:

· what they do in that club
· what time they meet or practise
· where they carry out the activities.

Club representatives should also ask visiting students what they are interested in to help them with their choice of clubs.

いってみましょう

⊗⊗ Mark and Emma are exchange students in 大館 and will attend Hoomei High School. In this conversation they are talking to Kumiko about the various ぶかつ or club activities displayed on the poster at the school.

マーク: ほうめい高校には、どんなスポーツのクラブが
　　　　あるの?

くみこ: マークくんはスポーツがすき?スポーツのクラブは
　　　　たくさんあるよ。ポスターを見て。

マーク: これはけんどうクラブ?

くみこ: うん、けんどうぶ。

マーク: ぶ?

くみこ: うん、クラブは日本語で「ぶ」。

マーク: へえ?じゃ、サッカークラブはサッカーぶ?

くみこ: そうよ。

マーク: サッカーぶはよくれんしゅうするね。

くみこ: そうね。そして、時々日よう日にしあいをするよ。
　　　　やきゅうぶはまいしゅう日よう日にしあいをするよ。

マーク: へえ!?これは Athletic Club だね。日本語で何?

くみこ: りくじょうぶ。

エマ: これ、ピンポンぶ?

くみこ: ちがう、ちがう。たっきゅうぶ。エマさんは
　　　　ぶんかぶとスポーツぶ、どっちがすき?

エマ: わたし、ぶんかぶのほうがいい。あっ、この
　　　　しゃしん、くみこさん?

くみこ: うん。わたし、えい語ぶに入ってるの。

エマ: ぶんかぶはどんなクラブがあるの?

くみこ: ええと、かがくぶ、びじゅつぶ、えい語ぶ、
　　　　しょどうぶ、かどうぶ、さどうぶ...

エマ: しょどう?かどう?さどう?むずかしいね。

くみこ: そうね。しょどうは calligraphy、かどうは flower
　　　　arranging、さどうは tea ceremony。

マーク: へえ?おもしろそうだね。ぼくもさどうぶに入れる?

くみこ: うん、もちろん。

マーク: れんしゅう日は何よう日?

くみこ: ええと、金よう日の四時から五時まで。二かいの
　　　　ぶんかしつで。

エマ: わたしはフルートができるの。

くみこ: じゃ、ブラスバンドぶに入る?

エマ: うん、そうする。どこでれんしゅうするの?

くみこ: おんがくしつで。
　　　　エマさん、がんばってね。

単語 (dialogue)	
ポスター	poster
れんしゅうする	to practise
ぶんか	culture
(クラブ)に入ってる	to be in (a club, team etc.)
ぶんかしつ	a classroom for cultural activities
フルート	flute

単語 (poster opposite)	
練習日	practice day(s)
場所	venue
ラボ	language laboratory

クラブかつどう

わたし、テニス部に入ってるの。

* 陸上部
練習日　月、水、金
時間　　4:00 から 6:00
場所　　大館陸上グランド

* 卓球部
練習日　火、木、土
時間　　火、木:
　　　　4:00 から 5:30
　　　　土：1:00 から 3:00
場所　　体育館

* 剣道部
練習日　月、水
時間　　4:30から 7:00
場所　　体育館

* サッカー部
練習日　男：月、水、金、
　　　　土
　　　　女：火、木、土
時間　　月～金：
　　　　3:45 から 6:30
　　　　土：1:00 から 3:30
場所　　校庭

* 美術部
練習日　土
時間　　1:00 から 4:00
場所　　美術室

* 化学部
練習日　木
時間　　3:45 から 5:00
場所　　化学室

* 英語部
練習日　火、木
時間　　4:00 から 5:00
場所　　ラボ

* ブラスバンド部
練習日　月、火、木、金
時間　　4:00 から 5:30
場所　　音楽室

* 華道部
練習日　水
時間　　4:00 から 5:00
場所　　文化室

* 茶道部
練習日　金
時間　　4:00 から 5:00
場所　　文化室

* 書道部
練習日　木
時間　　4:00 から 5:30
場所　　3A

Crafted with pride in the lumpy gravy?! Well, really! It doesn't make a lot of sense, does it? When you see signs like this in Japan - and you do see them all over - you feel like rushing up to the owner of the shop and protesting, 'That sign out there, it doesn't mean anything!'

But don't bother. The owner knows it doesn't make sense, and he doesn't care. He doesn't want a proper sentence, he doesn't want meaning, he wants to create an effect, he just wants a 'look'. You can laugh all you like at the lumpy gravy man's sign and he will grin along with you: へんだね.

You take a T-shirt from the rack and read, *Balloon Boy. Unrestricted for the naughty boys. Since 1964.* The one next to it reads, *Nice feeling and crossover life. Young at heart. Fighting spirit. Second mind games.* Nonsense! You might laugh, or you might start getting frustrated that you are reading perfectly good English words assembled in perfectly ridiculous combinations.

But don't get frustrated. The English on these garments is part of an overall fashion statement, and fashion statements don't have to make sense, at least not in the way ordinary statements do. There is more to language than just meaning. There is sound (people say they like or dislike the sound of languages they don't understand) and there is shape. It is the shape of the English letters, words and 'sentences' that helps create the right look for the fashion-conscious. Japanese designers and advertising people are not silly. They could produce sensible English sentences if they wanted to. But that's just not the point.

Language is bound up with culture. If English-speaking (particularly American) culture has prestige, then the language has prestige too. The language on a T-shirt connects the wearer with an exotic, far-off land, giving them an imagined share of that culture. Fashion and fantasy always go together.

People use language in this way all over the world. In English speaking countries, French and Italian words and phrases have been designed into clothes to give extra sophistication. At different times kanji characters have been all the rage. People don't really care what the characters mean, they probably don't even care if the kanji are the right way up!

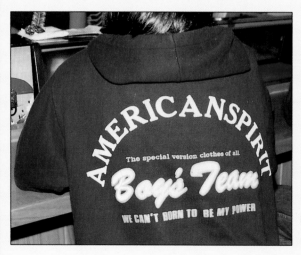

入

Meaning: *enter, go in*

Readings
はい (る)、いり

入る・はいる
入って・はいって
入れる・はいれる
入口・いりぐち

出

Meaning: *leave, go out*

Readings
で (る)、で (かける)

出る・でる
出かける・でかける
出口・でぐち

口

Meaning: *mouth*

Readings
くち、ぐち

口・くち
山口さん・やまぐちさん
出口・でぐち
入口・いりぐち

一 Deciding between two things

When you are asking which of two things your friend likes or prefers, you first of all say the two things, joined by と, and then ask which is better.

e.g. カーキーのときいろいのの、
どっちがいい?
   Which are better: the khaki ones or the yellow ones?

To ask this question in polite speech, it is necessary to line up the two items using と after each one and then ask which is preferred using どちら, the polite form of どっち.

e.g. 300円のと400円のとどちらがすきですか。
   Which do you prefer: the one for 300 yen or the 400-yen one?

も is used after どっち and どちら when you like both things.

e.g. どっちもいいね。
   Either is OK.

   どちらもすきですね。
   I like both.

To say that you prefer something, you use (の)ほう after the item you like.

e.g. ピンクのほうがすき。
   I like the pink one better.

   すしのほうがいいですね。
   Sushi would be better.

For い adjectives, you do not have to put の before ほう.

e.g. あかいほうがすきです。
   I prefer the red one.

You can only use どっち (or どちら) and ほう when you are deciding between two things.

より means *than* and you can use this to give more emphasis to your choice.

e.g. にくよりさかなのほうがすきです。
   I like fish better than meat.

When you use より to emphasise, note that it comes at the beginning of the sentence.

二 The biggest and the best

To say that something is the biggest or the most expensive, you put 一ばん before the adjective.

e.g. このとりいは日本で一ばん大きいです。
   These are the biggest tori gates in Japan.

どれ means *which* when you are comparing or deciding from among more than two things. To ask which is the best, you use the expression どれが一ばんいい?

e.g. しろいのとチェックのとくろいの、
どれが一ばんいい?
   Out of the checked one, the white one and the black one, which is the best?

There are various ways to respond to this.

e.g. ぜんぶいい。
   They're all good.

   ぜんぶよくない。
   None are any good.

   しろいのが一ばんいい。
   The white ones are the best.

In polite speech, of course, you will need to add です to these questions and responses.

どれが一ばんすき? これ!

はいく is a traditional form of Japanese poetry which is still very popular in Japan and has caught on in many countries around the world.

The はいく writer aims to communicate a single strong impression or to give a fleeting glimpse of a small corner of life. The poet's words drop onto the page like pure crystals.

Originally, はいく dealt in seasonal images but, as the examples below illustrate, today's はいく writer may write about any area of his or her experience. The challenge is to express this meaning according to a strict pattern: はいく poetry consists of 17 syllables, arranged in three lines of five, seven and five syllables. If you read out one of your はいく to a Japanese person they may count off the syllables on their fingers as you recite ― just to make sure you are following the rules.

In most はいく the last line has the most impact, often because it comes as a surprise. The poem just didn't seem to be going in that direction!

Your insights into life are just as valuable as anyone else's, so take up the challenge, become a はいく writer yourself, become a founding member of your school's はいく club. Liberate the poet in you! All you have to remember is 五, 七, 五.

なつやすみ
あさねぼうする
おひるまで

きっさてん
おなかペコペコ
ダイエット

いそがしい
みせでのバイト
おかねすき

うたじょうず
みんなうたおう
カラオケへ

単語

単語	
うどん	noodles
おなじ	same
こい	carp
こおり	ice, shaved ice dessert
今年(ことし)	this year
さいしょ	the first
それでも	and yet
どこも	everywhere
どちら／どっち	which (of two)
どれ	which (of more than two)
二ばんめ	the second
ヤツ	fellow, guy
...より	than...

Verbs	
つかれる	to become tired
つく	to arrive
(...に)つとめている	to work for
もらう	to receive
びっくりする	to be surprised

Expressions	
いいですか	are you ready?
とらないで	don't take it
もちろん	of course

Locations	
いけ	pond
かいしゃ	firm, company
きっさてん	coffee shop, tearoom
せかい	world
そと	outside
ちゅうしゃじょう	car park

外来語 (がいらいご)	
チャンピオン	champion
ハイテクな	high tech
ヘアカット	hair-cut
パーマコース	types of available hair perms
ラグビーシャツ	rugby top
ロサンジェルス	Los Angeles

あ

アイスクリームスタンド	ice cream stand
あいたくて	want to see (a person) and...
あいている	to be vacant
あえる	can meet
あげる	to give
あさ	a.m.
あさねぼうする	to sleep in, to sleep late
あそばないで	don't play up!
あそびに来る (くる)	to come and visit
アトラクション	attraction
ある	to be located, there is
ある日 (あるひ)	one day
アルバイト	part-time job

い

いいアイディアだね	that's a good idea!
いいですか	are you ready?
いいなあ	lucky you!
いけ	pond
いそがしい	busy
いし	rock, stone
いしゃ	doctor
一ばん	first, number one
いっぱい	full
イベント	event
いろいろ(な),いろんな	various

う

ううん	uh uh, no
うけつけ	receptionist
うどん	noodles
うらやましい	envious, jealous
...うりば	...sales area
うる	to sell
うれしい	happy, pleased
うん	yeah
うんてんしゅ	driver

え

えきいん	station employee
えきべん	べんとう purchased at stations
エキサイティング	exciting
エコノミールーム	economy room

SF (エスエフ)	science fiction
えま	wooden tablet to write wishes on

お

おい	my nephew
おいごさん	your nephew
おおあたり	a big win
お金 (おかね)	money
おくじょう	rooftop
おこのみやき	a kind of thick, spicy pancake containing vegetables and meat or seafood
(お)しごと	work, job
おじ	my uncle
おじさん	your uncle
オス	hi!
おそい	late
おてら	Buddhist temple
おとこのこ	boy
〜のオーナー	...owner
おなかすいた	I'm hungry
おなかペコペコ	I'm starving!
おなじ	same
おにぎり	riceball/s
おねがい!	please!
(お)ひるごはん	lunch
おば	my aunt
おばさん	your aunt, lady, woman
(お)べんとう	packed lunch
おまわりさん	neighbourhood policeman
おみくじ	written fortune
おみまい	visiting someone who is sick/injured
おわる	to end, to finish
おんなのこ	girl

か

カーキー	khaki
が	but
ガールフレンド	girlfriend
かいけいし	accountant
ガイド	tour guide
かいしゃ	firm, company
かいしゃいん	company employee
かえす	to return something
買える	can buy, to be able to buy
かかる	to take time
かく〜	each, every
カスタードクリーム	custard-filled doughnuts

カセット	cassette
ガソリンスタンド	petrol station
かたち	shape
かつ	to win
がっかりしちゃう	I am so disappointed! What a blow!
かっこう	appearance, look
かど	corner
かよう	to commute, to go
かりる	to borrow, to rent
から	from
カラフル	colourful, bright
かわいそう	poor you! poor thing!
かんごふ	nurse
がんばる	to try hard

き

きしゃ	train (for long distances)
きっさてん	coffee shop, tearoom
木(き)にむすぶ	to tie on a tree
きもちいい	this is great!
キャンペーンガール	campaign girl
キャンペーンボーイ	campaign boy
ぎりの...	...in-law, step...
ぎんこう	bank
ぎんこういん	bank employee

く

グーグー	zzz!
〜ぐみ	...class
ぐらい	about, approximately (after amount)
クラブのせんぱい	senior student in a club
クラブのメンバー	member of a school club
グリーン	green
くりかえし	repeat

け

けいかん	police officer
けいざい	economics
けしき	scenery
けっこんしている(しています)	to be married
けど	but
けんちくか	architect

こ

こい	carp
こうしゅうでんわ	public phone
こうちょうせんせい	school principal
こうむいん	public servant
こおり	ice, shaved ice dessert
ゴールデンウィーク	Golden Week
こく語	Japanese language
ごちゅうもんは?	your order?
コック	cook
こっち	here
今年 (ことし)	this year
子ども (こども)	child/children
子どもさん (こどもさん)	your children
子どもの日 (こどものひ)	Children's Day
来なかった (こなかった)	didn't come
このへん	around here, in this vicinity
コメディー	comedy
ごめん	sorry
ごりょうしん	your parents
これから	and now, from now
こわい	scared, scary
コンテスタント	contestant
コンテスト	contest
こんど	next
こんばん	tonight
コンピューター	computer

さ

サーフィン	surfing
さいしょ	the first
サイズ	size
さくら	cherry blossoms
(じゅぎょうを)サボる	to skip (classes)
さむくて	cold and...
サンキュー	thank you
ざんねん	that's bad luck/how disappointing
サンドイッチ	sandwich

し

しあい	match, game
しか	deer
しかたがない	that's too bad, it can't be helped
しごと	work, job

~時間目 (じかんめ)	counter for school periods or classes
時間わり (じかんわり)	timetable
じきゅう	hourly rate
しつもん	question
じどうはんばいき	vending machine
しま	island
しましま(の)	striped
ジャスコ	name of a department store
ジャンボポテト	baked potato
ジュース	juice, soft drink
じゅぎょう	class
しゅふ	housewife
じゅんびする	to prepare
ショー	show
しょくじつき	meal provided
ショッピングセンター	shopping centre
(お)しろ	castle
しんごう	traffic lights
じんこう	population
じんじゃ	Shinto shrine
しんじられない	I don't believe this...

す

すいどうや	plumber
スコア	score
スキーツアー	skiing holiday
すこし	a bit
すみません	thank you
スタジオ	studio
スナック	snack
スリル	thrill

せ

せかい	world
ぜんぜん	not at all
(お)せんべい	cracker biscuit

そ

そうしよう	let's do that
そうすると	after that, then...
(お)そうじ	cleaning
そうじする	to do the cleaning
そと	outside
そつぎょうしき	graduation ceremony
そのつぎ	after that
そば	beside, near
それでも	and yet
そんなに	not that much

た

たいいくさい	annual sportsday
ダイエット中 (ちゅう)	on a diet
大学 (だいがく)	university
大学生 (だいがくせい)	university student
だいたい	generally, mostly
たいてい	usually
たいへん	how awful!
だから	therefore
だけ	only, just
タクシーのうんてんしゅ	taxi driver
タクシーのりば	taxi stand
だった	was
たのしみにしている	to look forward to
たまご	egg
田んぼ	rice field

ち

チェック(の)	checked
ちゃんと	perfectly, properly
ちゅうしゃじょう	car park
ちがう	no, (that's not the reason)
ちかいっかい	basement
ちかにかい	second floor basement
チキン	chicken
チケットうりば	ticket box
ちょっと	it's a bit...
チンジャラジャラ	the sound of *pachinko*

つ

つかれる	to become tired
つく	to arrive
つとめている	to work for...
つれて	take someone

て

テイスト	taste
ディスコ	disco
デートする (します)	to go on a date
でかけないで	don't go out!
出口 (でぐち)	exit
デラックスルーム	deluxe room
テレホンカード	telephone card
出る (でる)	to leave

(コンテスト) に出る (でる)	to enter (a contest)
てん	point
てんいん	shop assistant
でんきや	electrician

と

とおい	far
トイレ	toilet
どうもごちそうさま	thank you very much
どうやって行く	how will you get there?
とくべつ(な)	special
どこも	everywhere
どっち／どちら	which? (of two)
どのぐらい	how long?
とらないで	don't take it
トランプ	playing cards
トランプする	to play cards
とりい	Shinto gateway
トリプル	triple (ice cream)
どれ	which? (of more than two)
トロフィー	trophy
トンネル	tunnel

な

ない	there isn't
ないしょ	secret
なくなる (なくなります)	to die
何か (なにか)	something
何かい (なんかい)	what floor?

に

二ばんめ	the second
にゅうじょうけん	admission ticket

ね

ねがいごと	prayer or wish
ねられる	to be able to sleep
～ねんまえ	...years ago

の

のどかわいた	thirsty
(そうじした)のに...	I've even (cleaned up)
のみもの	drink
のりたい	want to ride in

は

ハーイ	hi!
ハロー	hello
バースデー	birthday
パーマコース	types of available hair perms
はいしゃ	dentist
(クラブ)に入ってる (はいってる)	to be in (a club, team, etc)
ハイテク(な)	high tech
バイト	part-time job
ばか	don't talk rubbish!
はし	bridge
はじまる	to begin, to start
はじめまして	pleased to meet you
ばしょ	venue
バスてい	bus stop
はたち	20 years of age
...はどこでしょうか	can you tell me where ... is?
バナー	banner
はなせる	can speak
はなみ	cherry blossom viewing, flower viewing
ハニーディップ	honey-dipped doughnuts
はらう	to pay
パレード	parade
バンド	band
ハンドラー	handler

ひ

ひしょ	secretary
びっくりする	to be surprised
一つめの...	the first...
(お)ひるごはん(に)	(for) lunch
左 (ひだり)	left
左がわ (ひだりがわ)	left-hand side
一人で	by myself
びょういん	hospital

ふ

ファンタスティック	fantastic
フィーリング	feeling
フィルム	film (photographic)
フェリー	ferry
二つめの...	the second...
ぶつり	physics
ふゆ	winter
ブラスバンド	brass band

プライズ	prize
プラモデル	plastic model
フランク	frankfurt
フルート	flute
ぶんか	culture
ぶんかしつ	a classroom for cultural activities

へ

ヘアカット	hair-cut
へいわこうえん	Peace Park (in Hiroshima)
ベージュ	beige
べつに	nothing in particular, nothing much
べんごし	lawyer
(お)べんとう	packed lunch
べんり(な)	handy, convenient

ほ

ほうかご	after school
ぼうし	hat
ボーイフレンド	boyfriend
ぼくたち	we (males)
ぼくのじゃないです	it's not mine
ポスター	poster
ポスト	post-box
ポップコーン	popcorn
ほんと	really

ま

まあまあ	so-so
～まい	counter for thin, flat objects
マイクもって	holding the microphone
まいこさん	apprentice *geisha*
まがる (まがります)	to turn
まける	to lose, to be defeated
まじめ(な)	conscientious, serious
まっすぐ	straight, straight along
まった?	have you been waiting long?
まったく	really! you always say that!
まで	until, up to, as far as, to

み

見える	to be able to see
右 (みぎ)	right
右がわ (みぎがわ)	
	right-hand side
みずたま(の)	spotted
みち	street, road
みんなで	altogether, with everyone

む

むねがドキドキする	
	to have one's heart beat madly
むらさき	purple

め

めい	my niece
めいごさん	your niece
(うたの)メニュー	list of available songs

も

モカ	mocha flavour
もちろん	of course
もらう	to receive
もらえる	to be able to receive, can receive
もん	gate

や

や	and
やきとり	pieces of chicken on skewers
やすみ	holiday, rest
ヤツ	fellow, guy
山のぼり	mountain climbing
ヤング	young

ゆ

ゆうしょうする	to win the championship
ゆうびんきょく	post office
ゆき	snow
ゆきあそび	playing in the snow
ゆっくり	slowly, leisurely
ユニフォーム	uniform

よ

ようちえん	kindergarten
ようふく	clothes
...より	than...
よる	p.m.

ら

らく	easy, comfortable
ラグビーシャツ	rugby top
ラジカセ	radio-cassette player
ラボ	language laboratory

り

| りょうしん | parents |
| りょこうする | to travel, to take a trip |

れ

れんしゅうする	to practise
れんしゅう日 (び)	
	practice day(s)

ろ

ロープウェー	ropeway
ロサンジェルス	Los Angeles
ロマンス	romance
ロマンティック(な)	
	romantic

わ

わかる?	do you understand?
わからない／わかんない	
	I don't understand
わすれる	to forget
わたる (わたります)	
	to cross

単語・英語・日本語

A

a.m.	あさ
accountant	かいけいし
after school	ほうかご
after that	そのつぎ
after that, and then	そうすると
ago	...まえ
alone, by myself	ひとりで (一人で)
altogether	みんなで
and now	これから
and yet	それでも
and	と, や
appearance	かっこう
approximately	～ぐらい
architect	けんちくか
around here	このへん
to arrive	つく
aunt (mine)	おば
(yours)	おばさん

B

band	バンド
brass band	ブラスバンド
bank	ぎんこう
bank employee	ぎんこういん
banner	バナー
to become tired	つかれる
to begin, to start	はじまる
beige	ベージュ
beside, near	そば
a bit, a little	すこし
to borrow	かりる
boy	おとこのこ
boyfriend	ボーイフレンド
bridge	はし
builder	だいく
bus stop	バスてい
busy	いそがしい
but	が, けど

C

car park	ちゅうしゃじょう
carp	こい
carpenter	だいく
cassette	カセット
castle	(お)しろ
champion	チャンピオン
checked	チェック(の)
cherry blossom	さくら
chicken	チキン

(child)

child, children (mine)	こども (子ども)
(yours)	こどもさん
Children's Day	こどものひ (子どもの日)
...class	～ぐみ
class, lesson	じゅぎょう
cleaning	そうじ
to do the cleaning	そうじする
clothes	ようふく
club member	クラブのメンバー
club senior student	クラブのせんぱい
coffee shop, tearoom	きっさてん
colourful	カラフル
to come and visit	あそびにくる (来る)
comedy	コメディー
to commute	かよう
company, firm	かいしゃ
company employee	かいしゃいん
computer	コンピューター
conscientious	まじめ(な)
contest	コンテスト
contestant	コンテスタント
convenient	べんり(な)
cook	コック
corner	かど
counters flat things	～まい
floors	～かい
hours	～じかん (時間)
minutes	～ふん／ぷん (分)
school periods	～じかんめ (時間目)
cracker biscuit	(お)せんべい
to cross	わたる (わたります)
culture	ぶんか

D

to go on a date	デートする
deer	しか
dentist	はいしゃ
diet	ダイエット
on a diet	ダイエットちゅう (中)
to die	なくなる
disappointing	ざんねん
I'm disappointed	がっかりしちゃう
disco	ディスコ
doctor	いしゃ
drink	のみもの

E

each	かく～
easy, comfortable	らく
economics	けいざい
egg	たまご
electrician	でんきや
to end	おわる
to enter (a contest)	(コンテストに)でる (出る)
envious	うらやましい
event	イベント
everywhere	どこも
exit	でぐち (出口)

F

far	とおい
fellow, guy	ヤツ
ferry	フェリー
film (photographic)	フィルム
first	一ばん
flower viewing	はなみ
flute	フルート
to forget	わすれる
fortune paper	おみくじ
from	から
full	いっぱい

G

gate	もん
gateway (Shinto)	とりい
generally	だいたい
girl	おんなのこ
girlfriend	ガールフレンド
to give to someone	あげる
graduation ceremony	そつぎょうしき
great!	きもちいい
green	グリーン

H

hair-cut	ヘアカット
handy	べんり(な)
happy	うれしい
hat	ぼうし
hello	ハロー
here	こっち
high tech	ハイテク(な)
hi	オス、ハーイ
holiday	やすみ
hospital	びょういん
hourly rate	じきゅう

単語

● 百五十